Work and organizations

INTRODUCTIONS TO SOCIOLOGY

Work and organizations

Edward Webster

Sakhela Buhlungu

Andries Bezuidenhout

OXFORD
UNIVERSITY PRESS

OXFORD
UNIVERSITY PRESS

Great Clarendon Street, Oxford OX2 6DP

Oxford University Press is a department of the University of Oxford.
It furthers the University's objective of excellence in research, scholarship,
and education by publishing worldwide in

Oxford New York

Auckland Bangkok Buenos Aires Cape Town Chennai
Dar es Salaam Delhi Hong Kong Istanbul Karachi Kolkata
Kuala Lumpur Madrid Melbourne Mexico City Mumbai
Nairobi São Paulo Shanghai Taipei Tokyo Toronto

Oxford is a registered trade mark of Oxford University Press
in the UK and certain other countries

Published in South Africa
by Oxford University Press Southern Africa, Cape Town

Work and organisations
ISBN 0 19 578077 9

© Oxford University Press Southern Africa 2003

Commissioning editor: Arthur Attwell
Editor: Ken McGillivray
Indexer: John Linnegar
Designer: Kerry + Krynauw
Cover designer: Christopher Davis
Illustrators: Kerry + Krynauw

Published by Oxford University Press Southern Africa
PO Box 12119, N1 City, 7463, Cape Town, South Africa

Set in 9 pt on 12 pt ITC Garamond Light by Orchard Publishing
Reproduction by Castle Graphics
Cover reproduction by The Image Bureau
Printed and bound by Clyson Printers, Maitland, Cape Town

Contents

Introduction to the Series

This small book forms part of a series of small books. The series aims to present basic sociology in a somewhat different way. First, it presents foundational sociological topics in modular form, that is each topic is presented in a separate book. That gives them considerable flexibility. Topics can be variously combined to fit a wide spectrum of introductory courses. No longer will you need to buy a hugely expensive 400-page textbook of which you use only one quarter of the available chapters. With this series you can buy exactly what you want and use all of it. The first six topics will offer introductions to: sociology in general, population studies, social institutions (education and the family), poverty and development, work and organizations, and crime and deviance.

Secondly, each book is written in such a way that it tells a coherent story with a developing and cumulative theme. Too many textbooks are accumulations of vaguely related concepts containing no discernible thread or structure. Our view in this series is that logical and sequential argument is one of the prime skills students learn at university level. As such, the texts they work with must model that style, and the exercises they do must practise it. In consequence it is important not only that the style of writing be lucid, logical, and organized, but also that the exercises in the book be geared towards higher cognitive skills. You will see that the exercises at the end of each book are carefully constructed to test a range of thinking skills. At the same time, there is absolutely no reason why such discussions cannot be clear and accessible, written in language that flows and entertains as it educates. Annotated bibliographies can further this aim by indicating those existing sociological works which promote a similarly easy and rich style.

Thirdly, the various books deal with issues of some substance in sociology. They go beyond the elementary concepts which make up a particular problem area. They introduce students to debates that are current and alive in modern sociology. Clearly, an introductory textbook cannot expose its readers to the full complexity of technical argument. Texts therefore need to build up gradually a repertoire of technical language and an armoury of concepts, as is the case in any discipline. After all, you cannot simply get into a car and drive it without knowing how its controls, instruments, and signals work. But once you have the hang of it, it can become a thing of great power.

Fourthly, there are many sociology teachers who want sociology textbooks to be more accessible to southern African students, to use southern African examples, and promote something called 'southern African sociology'. While sociological writing in this subcontinent without doubt benefits from the use of southern African references and examples, and this series of books certainly pursues that practice, the spread of ethnic or cultural groups and ideological convictions, makes the existence of a southern African sociology, in the singular, very doubtful. Rather we would expect a range of sociologies, in the plural. But, even then, the influence of global sociological paradigms is so powerful that it is difficult to find anything which could be called distinctively 'southern African'. So, southern African reference points and examples, yes, but southern African sociology(ies) – very difficult.

Finally, sociology is a discipline that can reveal, open up, unveil the social world around us in wondrous ways. Its like cracking a secret code. It can make unthought-of, even unheard-of, connections and links. But it can also be personal and challenging. It can put question marks behind some of your most dearly held beliefs. Going on the sociological journey, then, can be exciting, surprising, angering, outrageous, and scary. It would not be true sociology if it were not.

Johann Graaff
Series Editor

Introduction

This book is about work and the organizations which shape and are shaped by it. Work is about those activities that are essential to our material and physical existence, to our place in the world, and, in fact, to every aspect of human life. Work is a universal condition of human existence. As Karl Marx wrote many years ago,

> Let us begin by stating the first premise of all human existence, and therefore of all history; the premise, namely, that men [sic] must be in a position to live in order to be able to make history. But life involves before anything else, eating and drinking, a habitation, clothing, and many other things. The first historical act is thus the production of the means to satisfy these needs, the production of material life itself (Marx 1976: 449).

In spite of the importance of production, the study of work and employment has become less fashionable than it was 20 years ago. Questions of identity, of discourse, of cultural forms, of personal biography, of consumption are seen as more important than the world of work. But as Richard Brown argues,

> ... the availability of opportunities for employment, and the conditions under which people are employed, still have more impact on most individuals' chances than many other more fashionable concerns. Work and employment structure our lives and shape inequalities of condition and opportunity to a greater extent than most if not all other areas of social life (Brown 1997: 1).

Three phases in the social scientific study of work in South Africa can be identified:

- The first phase begins in the 1930s, when sociologists first attempted to understand the impact of rapid industrialization on the white community, and on Afrikaners in particular. It was known at the time as the 'poor white problem'. At the same time, but within very different disciplinary boundaries, anthropologists were studying the impact of the migrant labour system on rural African society.
- The second phase begins after World War II, when industrial psychologists – and later industrial sociologists and industrial anthropologists – embarked on microstudies of the workplace. The central concern of these social scientists was the factors affecting productivity such as labour turnover, morale, and monotony in industry. Some of these studies spread the notion that black workers were culturally different and, therefore, less productive. This could be described as a form of 'cultural racism'.
- The third phase begins in the 1970s when, under the impact of a surge of worker action and organization, South African sociologists fell under the spell of Braverman's classic study, *Labour and Monopoly Capitalism: The Degradation of Work in the Twentieth Century*. The rapid growth of labour process studies transformed the study of work in

South Africa, leading to a range of studies on skill formation, racism in the workplace, and to such things as Taylorism and Fordism, which we shall consider later (Webster 2002).

The opening up of South Africa and the southern African region's economy in the 1990s to international competition has revitalized the social scientific study of work. From being an issue largely of concern to the academic world, the world of work is now one of the key issues facing policymakers and managers in southern Africa. The questions of international competitiveness, workplace change, skill development, labour standards, employment equity, and job creation have become questions of national importance.

The world of work is being profoundly transformed by broader societal changes at the regional, national, and global level. It is increasingly difficult to understand and manage the challenges resulting from this at the micro and organizational levels alone. We need a broader understanding of societies and economies. The international trend has been to widen the traditional notion of industrial sociology to cover all aspects of work, employment and unemployment and their connections with wider social processes and social structures.

This book goes beyond the workplace to focus on issues such as the informal economy and unpaid labour. It also goes well beyond traditional trade union organization to include other social movements. There are three parts: chapter 1 focuses on work, chapter 2 on bureaucracy and organizations, and chapter 3 on trade unions and movements.

Three broad themes underlie this book. The first theme is the way in which sociology emerges as a discipline to understand the damaging and dehumanizing effect of European industrialization. In *What is sociology?*, the first book in this series, the classical social theorists were introduced. In this book we draw on these theorists, and on Marx in particular, to show how the workplace is constantly restructured as employers compete with each other in their search for markets and profits. We identify four phases of capitalist development and show how the workplace is an arena of constant struggle between capital and labour.

The second theme, by contrast, focuses on Weber's notion of rational and efficient bureaucracy and the critiques of this approach by sociologists such as Gouldner and Burawoy. Again, the theme of this section is the need to recognize the importance of conflict rather than of social order as the driving force of capitalist development.

The third theme focuses on trade unions as a counterforce to managerial control and bureaucracy in the workplace. We demonstrate the tension between unions as organizations and as social movements. This theme draws on the work of Michels, and underlines the need to locate work and organizations in the context of an ongoing process of transformation.

We emphasize this theme in the final chapter when we discuss the future of the workplace and trade unionism. Has globalization created a completely different world driven by information technology? Or are we simply experiencing a new phase of capitalism, what some call 'imperialism', where the multinationals of the North continue to dominate the developing world of the South?

Work is still one of the basic determinants of how we live our lives.

We conclude the book by suggesting that globalization is a contradictory and uneven process that has created 'new winners' – those who have the capital and skills to *connect* to the global economy – and 'losers'. The losers are those who are *disconnected* from informational capitalism and are increasingly marginalized and socially excluded. Importantly, the large bulk of losers in the world are in Southeast Asia, Central and South America, and sub-Saharan Africa. The challenge facing students of society in the twenty-first century is to develop ways of understanding these processes so that all peoples benefit from the exciting technological innovations that increasingly shape the modern workplace.

1 Work

In the struggle between employers and workers, the organization of work went through a number of different phases. Each phase brought with it higher levels of productivity and new forms of control over labour. At the same time, it also enabled new forms of worker resistance.

Introduction

In this chapter we argue that there is a need to rethink the definition of work to include those unpaid activities in the household and the informal sector largely undertaken by women. The informal sector is that kind of economic activity which is not regulated by rules and laws, such as street trading. We argue that work needs to be understood historically and we draw a distinction between work in a pre-capitalist society and work in a capitalist society. We then show how work is progressively transformed as employers seek to increase productivity. We identify four phases in the transformation of work. The chapter concludes by suggesting that the last phase in the transformation of work has undermined the organizational base of industrial unions through the spread of casual work. However, it has also opened up opportunities for new forms of resistance.

Rethinking work

In contemporary industrial society, the term 'work' seems to have a perfectly clear meaning. It is an activity where an individual puts in *effort* (manual, mental, and emotional) during a specific *time* in a particular *space*. For example, work means that one starts working at eight o'clock in the morning in an office or a factory and continues to do so for eight hours. Importantly, this effort is accompanied by a monetary *reward*, that is, a salary or a wage. This is illustrated in the example below.

Time	Eight hours
Space	Office Factory
Effort	Manual Mental Emotional
Reward	Salary Wage

In this understanding of work, it is easy to distinguish 'work' from 'play'. For example, most people would readily understand the difference between someone working as a cook in a restaurant, preparing a meal for a wage and a casual social gathering where a person cooks a meal to celebrate a friend's birthday. The one is for money; the other is for fun. Work, in other words, is *paid labour*.

The distinction is, of course, not so simple. Let us take another example. A mother rises early in the morning to prepare sandwiches for her children to eat at school and also prepares breakfast for her husband. She is not normally paid if she is a wife or mother and not a domestic worker. But is it work? Caring for children and maintaining the household we call 'social reproduction'. It is certainly not play!

Of course, it would be wrong to assume that every woman preparing breakfast for another person is constrained to do so by a sense of family obligation. She may prepare breakfast for a neighbour who is ill. In other words, it may be an act of voluntary social solidarity. Is this social activity work?

The point that emerges from these four examples – cooking a meal for money (either in a restaurant, in a factory or a home), cooking a meal for pleasure, preparing food for your family, or preparing a meal for your neighbour – is that these activities cannot be understood if we do not know why, where or for whom they are undertaken. That is, work can be understood only in relation to the specific social relations in which it is embedded. Whether a particular social activity is work or play depends on a specific social context.

Fig 1.1: Types of work

Production	Social reproduction
Wage work (cook in a restaurant)	Reproduction of oneself and others (mother engaged in childcare)
Self-employed (cooking at home to sell)	Voluntary acts of social solidarity (cooking for sick neighbour) Play (cooking for dinner party)

Source: These examples are drawn from Pahl (1984).

What we mean by the sociological study of work is the need to embed work in a specific set of social relations. We need, therefore, to rethink our definition of work, to widen it to include activities with no expectation of monetary reward. In other words, activities where people have a sense of obligation to the household, to their friends, or to their neighbours. This type of work we call 'social reproduction'. We define work, then, not only as the sphere of production but include also social reproduction.

Our definition of work, then, is *a social activity where an individual or group puts in effort during a specific time and space, sometimes with the expectation of monetary – or other kinds of – rewards, or with no expectation of reward, but with a sense of obligation to others*. This definition enables us to distinguish between work and play and, more importantly, to define those activities in the household, undertaken largely by women, as (unpaid) work.

> Work is not always a paid activity. It is something done with a sense of obligation.

Work in pre-capitalist society

To understand various types of work, work needs to be understood historically. To live, women and men have to work. Yet, people in the early days,
before colonialism in southern Africa, were not workers in the way we think of
workers today. Some individuals, such as chiefs, had privileges, but everybody
in these early times had the right to land, could rear cattle, could hunt game
in the veld and by these means an individual could live. In more formal terms,
these men and women had access to the *means of production*.

For most of the time, they worked for themselves or their families, and not for
somebody else. Work in these pre-colonial societies was embedded in society
(Polanyi 2001). Individual economic interest was not all-powerful as it was to
become with the rise of capitalism, where societies are controlled by markets.
Instead, reciprocity (mutual obligations towards each other) and redistribution
guided human behaviour.

Work was done by the household, where a strict sexual division of labour
existed: men tended the cattle and women tended the crops and worked in the
home. When the need arose for assistance, neighbours would combine people
from different homesteads into work parties (*ilima*). The dictionary definition
of work in Xhosa is *umsebenzi*, that is, not merely the physical execution of
work, but the fulfilment of a household or community obligation (Kuckertz
1990). The important point is that people in pre-colonial times lived on the
land and shared what they produced. We call this a *'redistributive mode of
production'*.

A few people specialized in craftwork, such as metal workers making hoes or
assegais, or pottery workers making cooking pots. Skills were often handed
down from parent to child, but anyone could learn the skill if they wished.
There were gold mines and jewellers at least seven centuries ago, north and
south of the Limpopo River. For example, at Thulamela near Polokwane mining
took place and jewellery was made. At Thulamela fragments of a Chinese vase
from the Ming Dynasty, over seven centuries old, was discovered as well as
glass beads from India. In other words, these were not static societies. They
produced more than they needed and traded across the globe.

Cattle were the centre of the economy; they were the means of production.
They could supply milk as well as meat and they could reproduce themselves. You could use their skins for clothing and the cattle themselves for
ploughing.

Pre-capitalist work
Work embedded in social relations
Surplus shared
Traditional obligation
Social solidarity

When we look at work today, we see a different picture. Most people do not have land or, if they do, it is not productive land. They have to work for a wage for someone else who owns the means of production – a factory, office, or mine. They have to work for someone who wants to make a profit out of their effort – someone who owns the means of production.

Work in capitalist society

The onset of capitalism in the 1800s meant that societies which had previously been composed of various types of agricultural workers, peasants, and self-employed artisans and craftsmen were very rapidly transformed into industrial societies. Here the factory and its work norms progressively transformed all areas of industrial work. Capitalism exists when the process of production is organized by a market in which commodities, including labour itself, are bought and sold according to standards of monetary exchange. The process of creating a labour supply is called 'proletarianization', that is, the historic process of separating the producer from the means of production, the transformation of peasant to worker. It was often a violent process. Under colonialism it involved conquest by a foreign country and various types of 'unfree' labour such as slavery, *inboekselings* (forced 'apprenticeship' of young children and women), sharecropping, and contract labour. Instead of the economy being embedded in social relations, as existed in pre-colonial society, social relations were now embedded in the market economy. This is what Karl Polanyi has called the 'Great Transformation' (2001).

How did this process come about? Sociology as a discipline emerged to answer this question. It was, if you like, the intellectual child of the Industrial Revolution. When the major early works which established sociology were being produced – from Karl Marx to Emile Durkheim, and Max Weber – a period covering the mid-nineteenth century to the early twentieth century, European society was being subjected to major changes wrought by industrialization.

The emergence of sociology was connected, Claus Offe argues, to the widespread concern with the social, economic, cultural, and moral effects of moving from a non-industrial to an industrialized society. The classic tradition of sociology shared the view that work is *the* fundamental social experience. Work, and the social relations structured around work, was seen as the central dynamic of modern industrial society (Offe 1985). Each of the classical writers approached this topic quite differently.

For Marx, certain political and social consequences followed. The most important of these were the various forms of *alienation* or subjective estrangement experienced by the worker. Workers were alienated, first, from the products they had created, then from full and effective relationships with their fellow-workers and employer, from their own labour, and, finally, from direct involvement in the political and cultural ordering of the society in which they lived.

The phenomenon of *rationalization* (that is the replacement of institutions based on traditions and values with institutions based on individual and instrumental interests) was the central concern of Max Weber. He associated capitalism with the emergence of rationalization and the extension of bureaucratic organizations. (This is discussed in greater detail in chapter 2.)

For Durkheim, rapid industrialization broke down traditional moral controls that existed in pre-industrial society, leaving individuals with a lack of meaning in their lives. This lack of social constraint on an individual he called 'anomie'.

Fig 1.2: Work in different societies

Sociologists	Pre-capitalist society	Capitalist society
Polanyi	Work embedded in social relations	Social relations disembedded in the market
Marx	Surplus shared	Surplus sold
Weber	Traditional obligations	Instrumental and individualistic relationships
Durkheim	Social solidarity	Anomie

The transformation of work under capitalism

Work under capitalism has a twofold objective: first to produce a product or service that can be sold as a *commodity* and, secondly, to derive a profit from the sale of that commodity. In order to make a profit, that is a surplus, it is necessary to produce commodities that are greater in value than the sum of the values of the commodities that are used to produce it. For example, to sell a shirt at R15, and make a profit of R5, the total costs of producing the shirt should not exceed R10.

Cost of production

Raw materials (cloth, buttons, etc)	=	R2
Machinery (the use of a sewing machine)	=	R5
Labour (wages for workers)	=	R3
Total cost of production	=	*R10*

In other words, the formula used to calculate the profit is:
Profit = Price of the shirt − Cost of production
    R5 = R15 − R10

These shirts that are sold in the marketplace are in competition with the shirts produced by other employers. In other words, each employer is trying to increase the sale of their shirts in relation to the price of shirts produced by other employers. The question is: how do employers increase the sale of their shirts and, therefore, their profit? One obvious way for employers to increase their profit is for them to decrease the costs of production.

We can distinguish between two different ways of decreasing costs: first, by getting workers to work harder or, secondly, by reorganizing work so that more shirts can be produced in the same time. The former goal can be achieved by lengthening the working day through overtime work or by getting people to work faster on an assembly line. We call this strategy the 'intensification of labour'. An alternative – smarter – strategy is to reduce the amount of labour time required to produce a shirt, either through the use of machinery/automation or by reorganizing work more efficiently. In this strategy one is raising the productivity of labour.

In order to remain competitive, work is constantly reorganized. Indeed, for Marx, the history of work under capitalism is a history of the steady transformation of work as employers search for ways to improve productivity. It is possible to identify four phases in the transformation of work from the nineteenth century onwards:
- the rise of the factory;
- the rise of scientific management;
- the rise of Fordism, and
- the rise of post-Fordism.

Remember that, although we have described these as historical phases, one phase does not always completely replace another. This process is more like the growth of an onion with new layers being added on to old ones. It is quite possible to find today examples of all four of these 'phases' existing next to each other. We shall see in the next chapter, for example, how the same applies to forms of organization.

We shall see also that, whereas Marx wrote largely about the first of these phases – the rise of the factory – it is other writers such as Braverman and Castells who have taken this analysis forward. In doing so, they have frequently criticized Marx for his excessive focus on the importance of production in explaining capitalism. We shall see that these other writers, in discussing production, also include cultural, political, and consumer elements in their explanations.

The rise of the factory

The capitalist organization of work changed continually as employers and workers struggled for control.

The creation of factories in nineteenth-century England overcame the control that workers had over their work in the early phases of capitalism through the *cottage* or *putting-out* system. Under this earlier system, the employer hired a 'middleman' who brought raw materials to a worker's household and collected the finished product at a set time. As a result, the employer had no way of compelling workers to do a specific number of hours of labour; they worked from home and the domestic craftsman was 'master' of his time – stopping or starting when he desired. This lack of supervision under the conditions of the cottage industry meant that the employer had no control over how much the worker worked per day. It was also easy for the worker to steal raw materials.

Fig 1.3: Cottage industry

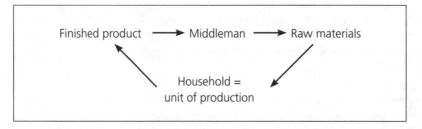

The factory was the central mechanism in securing control and lengthening the working day. By drawing all workers under one roof it increased management control through the introduction of supervisors and a system of 'clocking in'. Work was now done in a specific *space*, that is the factory, away from the household. It was also done during a specific period of time. In the words of Thompson (1963), 'Time was no longer *passed*, time was spent.' Time had become a *commodity* and, as a result, the first struggles in English factories were over the length of the working day.

Whereas the rise of the factory, said Marx, overcame some of the obstacles to profitability by bringing workers under direct employer control, it also created the opportunity for resistance to employers. It drew large numbers of men and women together under similar exploitative conditions. This facilitated communication between them and gave rise to collective action. Arising from these early forms of combination and collective action, trade unions were formed.

The function of the trade unions was to bargain collectively with employers in order to improve wages and working conditions (see chapter 3).

From Marx's point of view, then, capitalist production is centrally a contradictory process of cooperation and conflict. Some degree of cooperation is necessary for production to take place. At the same time a basic conflict exists between those who own the means of production and those who do not and have to sell their labour in order to survive. The source of this conflict lies in the fact that what is income for the worker, namely their wage, is a cost for the employer, which the employer naturally seeks to minimize. This is what makes the workplace an arena of contestation, a continuous power struggle over how much effort the worker has to make and for what reward.

Whereas the creation of the factory was an attempt to increase control over workers, the craftsmen still retained a degree of control over the content and performance of work. In the relentless drive for profits a further process of *deskilling* of the various work activities began. In this process crafts were broken down into a series of distinct, simpler tasks, thus introducing a division of labour and job fragmentation. While this process increased the productivity of labour, it had one crucial consequence for workers. Each worker's skill was diminished as his or her tasks became simpler. As a result less training was needed to perform the task efficiently, and it became easier for the employer to replace one worker with another. This was a huge step in the control that employers had over workers. From this point the Marxist history of transforming production is taken up by Harry Braverman (1974).

The rise of scientific management

Frederick Taylor, an engineer in the United States at the beginning of the twentieth century, was to raise the concept of 'control' to an entirely new plane when he asserted, as an absolute necessity for adequate management, the dictation to the worker of the precise manner in which work was to be performed (Taylor 1947). A major obstacle to the ability of employers to maximize the labour performed by their workers lay in the difficulty of knowing the time any particular piece of work actually took to be completed. The ability of workers to keep this knowledge from their employers formed the heart of the system of worker regulation of output, described by Taylor as 'soldiering'. Taylor and his 'efficiency experts' believed that, through a careful study of individual jobs and a careful selection of incentives and bonus pay, employers could structure the workplace so that soldiering could be eliminated. Management could strengthen its hand in the struggle to speed up production if it followed three principles that underlay what Taylor was misleadingly to call 'scientific management':

- Gather the *traditional skills* and experience (*tacit skills*) that workers possess and reduce them to a series of rules. Thus the first principle is to separate the knowledge that workers have from the workplace.
- To remove all brainwork from the shopfloor and put it in management's hands. As Taylor put it, 'You are not paid to think.'
- The third principle, then, is the use of this monopoly of knowledge to control each step of the work process and its mode of execution.

But scientific management came up against certain obstacles to control. The main problem faced by Taylorism is that workers attempted to subvert it. New struggles arose around the definition of skill and the process of deskilling. The introduction of machinery was to provide the structural solution to the obstacles faced by scientific management. With the introduction of machines instead of tools, production was freed from relying exclusively on human labour. The worker became a mere appendage of the machine. Under scientific management lengthening the working day and piecework generate increases in profits. Under machine-based production control over labour is once again more firmly in the hands of the employer.

The rise of Fordism

Fordism resulted in a dramatic rise in both the productivity of labour and the alienation of labour.

The introduction of machine-based production, said Braverman, leads to the replacement of craft skill (deskilling), the domination of man by machine, the separation of mental from manual labour, and the use of the machine as a weapon in the struggle between workers and employers. Managers would threaten to replace workers with machines, saying 'Machines don't go on strike, don't fall pregnant, and don't come to work babelaas (sic) (hung over) on Mondays'.

The process of increasing control over labour was taken further when Henry Ford inaugurated the first continuous assembly line for the Model T Ford in Detroit in January 1914, four years after Frederick Taylor's death. Within three months the assembly time for a Model T had been reduced to one-tenth of the time formerly needed and by 1925 Ford was producing almost as many cars in a single day as it had produced in an entire year. In Braverman's words:

> *The quickening rate of production depended not only on the change in the organization of labour but on the control which management, at a single stroke, attained over the pace of assembly, so that it could now double or triple the rate at which operations had been performed and thus subject its workers to an extremely intense form of work* (Braverman 1948: 148).

Fordism, as it became known, subjected the production process to the rule of speed. Ford put it simply, 'The ideal is the man must have every second necessary, but not a single unnecessary second' (Beynon 1973: 19). Fordism deepened and therefore surpassed Taylorism in the workplace by the application of two complementary principles: the integration of different parts of the labour process by a system of conveyors; and the fixing of the workers to jobs and positions determined by the assembly line. The individual worker thus lost all control over his or her work rhythm.

The Model T was trendsetting not only because of the use of the assembly line, but also for the way in which consumption was promoted as both a reward for and a stimulus to production. Ford paid his workers the high wage of US$5 a day in exchange for monotonous work. In this way Ford workers became rich enough to buy a cheap car, thus stimulating the demand for more Model Ts. In other words, Fordism is not only a form of mass production of goods; it is also a way of stimulating mass consumption. Put simply, *Fordism is mass production plus mass consumption.*

The rise of the Fordist mode of production generated unprecedented growth in particular advanced industrial countries. But just as the rise of the factory facilitated workers' resistance, so did Fordism facilitate a new form of worker resistance, militant industrial unionism. Fordism linked together the plant's work force so that when the line stopped, every worker necessarily joined the strike. In a large integrated manufacturing operation, such as motor-car production, a small group of militants could cripple an entire system by shutting down a part of the line. Thus Fordism took relatively homogenous (skilled and unskilled) labour and linked them together in production (Edwards 1979). The combination proved to be exceptionally favourable for building militant industrial unionism initially in the United States in the 1930s and 1940s, in Europe in the 1950s and 1960s, and in late industrializing countries such as South Korea, Brazil, and South Africa in the 1970s and 1980s.

Fordism's intensification of labour, however, had a destructive effect on the mental and physical life of workers. Subjection to a uniform but ever-increasing pace of work, combined with decreased resting time, immensely increases fatigue, nervous exhaustion, and stress-related disorders. Fordism, therefore, became associated with high levels of absenteeism, labour turnover, and personal alienation. These developments laid the ground for the development of new forms of labour organization, namely *post-Fordism.*

Before we move on to discuss post-Fordism, it is important to note that the notion of Fordism incorporates a particular idea of consumerism. Some discussions of Fordism also include the role of government planning in the notion of Fordism. (See the discussion of regulation theory in chapter 3 of *Poverty and Development*, a companion volume in this series.) This concept, then, is critical of Marx's strong focus on production in explaining how capitalism works, and it moves to bring in considerations of consumer behaviour, the role of government and politics, and the role of culture. This critique is extended in the work of Piore and Sabel, and Castells, which we consider below.

In the 1980s a new transformation of work began. Under the impact of new information technology, opportunities opened up for the internationalization of production. It became possible to break up the production process and produce the different components of a good in separate parts of the world. Furthermore, the dropping of tariff barriers created an increasingly international labour market.

The rise of post-Fordism

In the service industry control is now exercised over workers' appearance and their feelings.

According to Piore and Sabel, work organization is being restructured along much more flexible and less alienating lines. Production is currently organized according to outdated principles, which results in an inability to respond flexibly. The obstacle to further productivity is the rigidity of Fordism. The alternative is 'post-Fordism' (Piore & Sabel 1984).

This flexibility takes two forms. First, *functional flexibility* does away with rigid job descriptions so workers can perform a number of different tasks. This may involve increasing the number of skills a worker has (*multi-skilling*), or it may simply involve increasing the number of tasks to be done (*multi-tasking*). This development has led some writers to argue that post-Fordism is a more worker-friendly form of production. It involves a reversal of the deskilling trend that Braverman emphasized so strongly, and it involves greater levels of worker participation and consultation.

Secondly, *numerical flexibility* creates groups of workers who have no job security. Such workers are employed as temporary, contract, casual, or part-time workers to make the labour market more 'flexible'. This means that in times of greater production they can be brought into the workplace on temporary contracts and when production declines they can be pushed out. These more vulnerable, peripheral workers are often women or groups who are discriminated against, such as immigrants.

At the centre of the new work order, then, is the idea of a *dual labour market* divided between the core and the non-core. The core work force is, often, involved in the informational economy based on knowledge and innovation in the new industries of computers, telecommunications, and biotechnology. Quite often these so-called 'knowledge workers' focus on the design and conceptualization of the product and are based in the advanced industrialized countries.

However, the actual production of goods often takes place in 'sweatshops' in developing countries. It is subcontracted to production sites in the *export processing zones* (EPZs) of Southeast Asia. EPZs are specific sites created by governments to attract international companies to establish labour intensive industries. Companies located in these sites are granted special privileges such as tax concessions or the right to repatriate their profit. Such industries as clothing, footwear, food processing, and electronics depend on the availability of cheap, unprotected and, largely, female labour to remain globally competitive.

In sharp contrast to the idea that this new phase is characterized by high skill and participatory forms of work – what we have called 'post-Fordism' – critics have pointed out that the most common form of work in this new fourth phase is the growth of routine Taylorist service work, such as customer representatives in call centres. (A call centre is a communication hub which takes calls from all over the world for a particular company or for a particular purpose. The International Cricket Council, for example, set up a call centre in Johannesburg to handle global queries regarding the 2003 Cricket World Cup.)

This growing integration of the world – this compression of time and space as some sociologists describe it – has been termed *globalization*. At the heart of the globalization of production is a new form of competition that focuses on quality, innovation, and flexibility. For Manuel Castells, we have entered a new phase of capitalism, *informational capitalism*:

> At the end of the twentieth century, we are living through one of these rare intervals in history. An interval characterised by the transformation of our 'material culture' by the works of a new technological paradigm organised around new informational technologies (1996: 29).

This has created what he calls the 'network society'. For Castells the old was hierarchical, the new is based on moving, more horizontal networks. A network is a temporary collaboration between companies or parts of companies shaped around a particular project. Its shape and composition is driven by the needs of the project. When the project ends, the collaboration also ends, and a new network starts forming around a new project. While this network process gives enormous mobility and flexibility to management, it makes things very difficult for labour. In the network society, says Castells, labour becomes localized, disaggregated, fragmented, diversified, and divided in its collective identity.

Informational capitalism has, of course, not spread to every corner of the world. Some countries and some regions of countries are connected into the network society, some are not. For Castells, those that are not connected are left further and further behind in the development race.

We appear to have here a fourth stage – after the factory, scientific management, and Fordism – in the struggle between capital and labour, called 'informational capitalism'. For Castells the social relations of production have become 'disconnected' (1996: 475). Capital, he says, is able to move freely and invisibly through the Internet and email across the globe eroding the idea of labour as a collective actor. Workers are scattered and isolated in small and, sometimes hidden, workplaces concerned with individual survival. Who the owners are, who the managers are, who the producers are and who the workers are, becomes increasingly blurred in a production process that is spread geographically.

A critical part of the new post-Fordist economy is the service sector. Performance in the service sector accounts for 79 per cent of the jobs in the non-agricultural sector in the United States. Furthermore, more than the 90 per cent of the new jobs in 2000 were in the service sector, while the number of goods-producing jobs steadily declined. There are two kinds of jobs in the service sector: highly skilled knowledge work in the information sector; and the more routine service sector jobs, call-centre work and sales jobs. In particular we have seen the growth of jobs in which face-to-face or 'voice-to-voice' interaction is a fundamental part of the work. This interactive service work requires some sort of emotional labour. *Emotional labour* is 'the conscious manipulation of the worker's self-presentation, either to display feeling states and/or to create feeling states in others' (Macdonald & Sirianni 1996: 3).

Workers performing this kind of labour do not just have to account for their physical appearance. Their attitudes, moods and feelings are also subject to supervision. Indeed, the body itself becomes a contested terrain for labour control. Lan (2001) suggests that there are four dimensions of body control in the new economy:
- the exploited body (for example, standing behind the counter for a long time);
- the disciplined body (for example, smiling at customers);
- the mirroring body (for example, looking beautiful), and
- the communicating body (for example, manipulating your feelings).

The crucial difference between the service economy and Fordism is that the *form of control changes*. Under Fordist manufacturing the relationship is a binary one between management and labour. The customer is largely ignored. By contrast, in the service sector the customer is the key determinant shaping the workplace. In these jobs workers have to perform *emotional labour*, to smile, and not react aggressively to abusive behaviour. In other words, in the service economy, the relationship is a three-way one between employer, employee, and customer and not a two-way relationship only between employer and employee, as in the case of Fordism.

Fig 1.4: Fordist and post-Fordist relationships compared

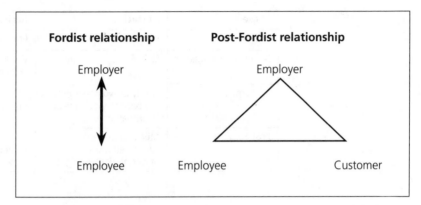

This last phase in the transformation of work, post-Fordism, has undermined the organizational base of industrial unions through the spread of casual work. However, whereas globalization has closed down opportunities for traditional trade union strategies, it has also created opportunities for new forms of resistance:

- First, multinational companies are being exposed to multinational bargaining pressures from an internationally coordinated labour movement.
- Secondly, the technological revolution brought about by globalization can be used to trade union activists' advantage. Email, web-sites, databases, and many other computer applications are being widely used around the world to find, store, analyse, and transmit information.
- Thirdly, we see the emergence of global norms of workplace rights: the notion that there are certain core labour standards that all societies must observe.

Conclusion

We have, then, identified four phases in the transformation of work in capitalist society:

- the rise of the factory;
- the rise of scientific management;
- the rise of Fordism, and
- the rise of post-Fordism.

At each phase in the transformation of work, employers attempted to overcome a series of obstacles to profitability. But each attempt by employers to extend control over work opened up new opportunities for workers to resist that control. The table below summarizes these two aspects of the history of work – obstacles, and resistance.

Fig 1.5: Aspects of the history of work

Phase	Obstacles	Resistance
The factory	Putting out system	Emergence of trade unionism
Scientific management	Skill of the craft worker	Workers contest definition of skill and resist deskilling
Fordism	Ability of workers to control the pace of work; militant industrial unionism	Militant shop floor-based unionism
Post-Fordism	Multinational, electronically connected resistance, universal workers' rights	Transnational trade union strategy linked to new social movements?

Organizations and Bureaucracy

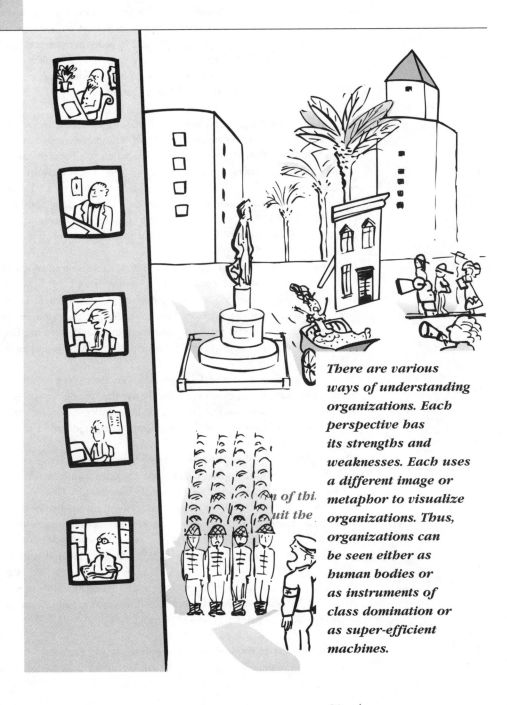

There are various ways of understanding organizations. Each perspective has its strengths and weaknesses. Each uses a different image or metaphor to visualize organizations. Thus, organizations can be seen either as human bodies or as instruments of class domination or as super-efficient machines.

Introduction

Our daily lives are shaped by many organizations. Some, such as the police, most schools, and the tax collector, are part of a constellation of organizations we call 'the state'. Others such as churches, trade unions, and pressure groups are formed by groupings of people who want to achieve certain shared goals. Then there are organizations that exist in order to make a profit for their owners or shareholders. Some of these business organizations are very small, but some have become known as 'multi-national corporations': or for example Coca-Cola, SABMiller, and the Ford Motor Corporation.

The fact that we confront so many of these organizations in our daily lives leads us to ask certain questions about them. These questions may result from a sense of frustration, or even desperation when we have to stand in long queues to pay car licence fees or municipal bills. This raises the question of organizational efficiency. Or a fuel company may attempt to build a petrol station in a suburb without taking into account its environmental impact. This raises questions about the power of major corporations and how citizens can assert their rights in opposition to these corporations.

In the South African context, on the other hand, attempting to progress beyond apartheid poses very real challenges for transformation. The South African Government has responded to this by passing an Employment Equity Act in 1998. This means that organizations have to reconsider, *inter alia*, the racial mix of their organizations and submit 'employment equity plans' to the Department of Labour, which is to approve and monitor progress made in this regard.

In turn, these attempts at social redress raise very interesting sociological questions about how societies change. We know that changing society is more difficult and complex than just introducing laws. Indeed, how do we approach organizational transformation? Can organizations change and, if so, how?

So, our experience of organizations raises questions of efficiency, of power, and of transformation. In this chapter we consider a number of sociological theories which help us to make sense of these issues. First, we investigate the systems approach to organizations often used by business managers. We contrast this with the critical approach which sees organizations as more conflictual, contested entities. We then move to consider Max Weber's classical treatment of bureaucracy as a clinically efficient machine, and the central role that it plays in modernity. Max Weber has over time elicited huge debate around the precise nature of bureaucracy, and its relationship to society and efficiency. We shall see that many writers today see organizations as moving beyond notions of machine-like bureaucracies.

Using metaphors to think about organizations is a fruitful way of broadening our vision of them. We have been speaking about Max Weber's image of an organization as a super-efficient machine. But organizations can also be thought of as organisms, as brains or as instruments of domination (Morgan 1997). As we move through various theories of organization we shall consider the images that they suggest about those organizations.

The systems approach

In the discussion that follows we consider two approaches to understanding organizations. One, called 'the systems approach', is quite close to functionalist theory. The other, called the 'critical approach', is similar to Marxist theory. We will show that, despite its link to functionalism, the systems approach does not take the broader societal context of organizations into account. The critical approach does. It also criticizes the systems approach for not recognizing that organizations are conflictual. That is to say, organizations are areas of contestation – terrains where different social classes and groupings struggle for control over resources. In contrast, Marxist critical approaches tend to overemphasize economic and power dimensions, while neglecting cultural aspects.

> A systems approach sees an organization as a body with various parts all under the control of a managerial head.

The systems approach often uses biological metaphors to describe organizations. As in a human body, an organization has a 'brain', 'eyes', 'hands', etc. Each part or 'sub-system' has its own function, and these different subsystems are coordinated by the managerial subsystem (Kast & Rosenzweig 1979). Organizations are seen to fulfil their functions successfully when they can sustain their existence by effectively transforming 'inputs' into 'outputs' much as a body might transform food into energy (Morgan 1997: 33). In the systems approach organizations have the following subsystems (see figure 2.1 below):

- The *managerial subsystem*, which is responsible for the overall direction of the organization and has to manage all the other subsystems in order to maintain organizational efficiency.
- The *structural subsystem*, which involves the way the different departments relate to each other in terms of hierarchy and work flow. Organograms are often used to describe how organizations are structured.
- The *technical subsystem*, which involves organizational equipment, machinery, and technical know-how.
- The *psycho-social subsystem*, which refers to the organizational values, culture, levels of motivation among staff, and commitment to organizational goals.
- The *environmental subsystem* which refers to the environment from which the organization draws its 'inputs' and to which the 'outputs' are deposited, be it in the form of goods or services (Kast & Rosenzweig 1979).

Fig 2.1: A systems approach to organizations

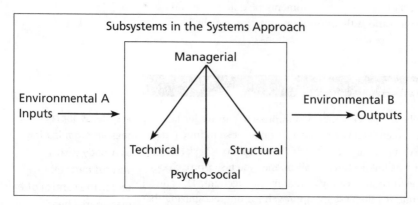

Staying with biological metaphors, organizations that do not successfully achieve their set goals by transforming 'inputs' into 'outputs', say the systems theorists, are considered to be 'sick'. But this can be cured by a 'scientific assessment' of the problem, which is usually located in one or more of the organizational subsystems. Management then decides on an 'intervention' strategy, which usually involves 'unfreezing' the organization, entering into a process of 'change management', and then 'refreezing' the corrected organization.

When employees question the organizational goals set by management, or form trade unions in the process, such a challenge to 'managerial preroga-tive' is seen as an organizational problem that has to be corrected. This raises a serious problem for systems analysis, since a common feature of social life – that of social conflict and contestation – becomes an 'organizational pathology', an 'illness'.

At the base of systems theory are a number of assumptions about how organizations actually operate (Kast & Rosenzweig 1979). Spelling out these assumptions will help us to be more critical about this approach. You will see how strong the links are to functionalist theory. These assumptions can be summarized as follows:

- First, system theorists assume that organizations are 'goal-seekers'. What distinguishes organizations from institutions (such as the family) and movements (such as the ecological movement) is that they are 'consciously created instruments' designed to achieve certain goals. The different parts of an organization (subsystems) work together to achieve these goals. They assume that there is value-consensus in any organization about organiza-tional goals.
- Secondly, they assume that 'rationally designed structures and practices resting on processes of calculated planning ... will maximize organizational effectiveness', that there is 'one best way' to achieve effectiveness.
- Thirdly, they assume that order and hierarchy are inherent in any organi-zation. This view sees organizations as 'cooperative social systems', which

tend towards 'a state of equilibrium'. They are 'unitary bodies' that combine 'the activities, values and interests of all their participants'. Management must ensure that there is order and hierarchy in the organization.

- Fourthly, they assume that management's version of rationality and efficiency is correct. Employees who oppose managerial decisions are seen 'to be acting irrationally, governed by a 'logic of sentiment''.
- Fifthly, this approach assumes that one can establish certain laws of organizational behaviour. It emphasizes the measurement of organizational processes, and argues that one can come to a general and universally true understanding of organizational practice and efficiency (Thompson & McHugh 1995).

The critical approach

Coming from a more Marxist angle, Thompson and McHugh (1995) do not like systems theory. In contrast, they present an image of organizations as instruments of domination. In this perspective, an organization is typically the tool which powerful members of society use to serve their needs. In such organizations workers are placed in positions of relative powerlessness where they are forced or subtly persuaded to do the bidding of the powerful (Morgan 1997: 301). Such an image suggests quite different assumptions.

The critical approach sees organizations as instruments through which one group dominates another.

First, when studying organizations, they say, it is important to question common-sense assumptions about how organizations operate. The systems approach sees the actions of managers as 'rational', and when workers challenge these actions, they are seen as 'irrational'. 'Instead of reflecting the concerns of established power-groups,' Thompson and McHugh (1995) argue, 'organizational theory should reflect critically on and challenge existing attitudes and practices'.

Secondly, for Thompson and McHugh, organizations are embedded in social structures. In the systems approach the 'organizational environment' is merely one factor that has an influence on how the organization operates as a system – in fact, sometimes 'the environment' merely becomes a 'subsystem' of the organization. Critical approaches, in contrast, understand the 'necessity to be *historical* and *contextual*'. Organizations are not 'free-floating or autonomous'. They are *embedded* in social structures. One cannot, for instance, understand gender inequality in an organization without taking into account the broader social structures and ideologies of patriarchy in which the organization is rooted.

Thirdly, in the critical approach, individuals who form part of organizations end up in specific positions (as 'managers' or as 'workers') largely because of their position in society. The systems approach tends to separate out the behaviour of workers in organizations from the position they are allocated to in the workplace. Industrial psychology is especially used to understand 'employee motivation' and 'organizational behaviour' as part of the 'psycho-social sub-system'. However, these approaches fail to take into account structures of domination in the organization, and how these structures relate to broader contours of social inequality outside of the organization. In order to understand this interplay between the individual worker and his or her position, a dialectical approach is required – an approach that can understand the process of negotiation between the individual and the collective.

Fourthly, in the view of the critical approach, the systems perspective sees organizations as harmonious and unitary entities. It is assumed that there is 'value consensus' as a basis for 'equilibrium'. However, there are always conflicts of interest between workers and managers, people in different departments, the organization, and other organizations or social groupings. Any social order established in an organization is therefore to a large degree the result of conflict and compromise, not value consensus. In order to understand the nature of organizations, it is important to recognize and explore these underlying social conflicts that stem from social inequality.

Fifthly, whereas mainstream approaches, such as the systems approach, have goals which are sympathetic to managers, critical approaches aim to bring about broad empowerment in the organizational context. Rationality in this context implies not narrow organizational rationality but an equitable distribution of power and resources in society more broadly.

In summary, the systems and critical approaches rerun many of the debates that functionalists have with Marxists in other areas of sociology. (See the discussion of the debate between these two theories in *What is Sociology?*, the first book in this series.) In the area of organizations also, each theory has its own strengths and weaknesses.

Max Weber: bureaucracy as an ideal type

For Weber, a modern bureaucracy operates like a well-oiled and precise machine.

As we saw in the previous section, many of the sociological approaches to the study of organizations share a concern about notions such as 'rationality' and 'efficiency'. Our sociological thinking about the nature or organizations has been substantially influenced by the work of the German social thinker, Max Weber (1864–1920). The concept 'bureaucracy' was developed by Weber in an attempt to understand the new social order that was establishing itself in Europe after the Industrial Revolution. Weber argued that as societies modernize organizations increasingly take on the form of bureaucracies. Weber saw modern bureaucracies as operating like clinical machines. In order to understand why Weber argued this, we have to analyse his theory of social action.

A theory of social action implies that we have to understand why people do certain things. In other words, we have to understand what meaning people find in their social actions, and what motivates them to act in certain ways. Now, this is in sharp contrast to the approach adopted by functionalism and Marxism. For both of these are macro-theories that argue for the strong influence of broad structures over individuals. Weber's theory of social action is a micro-theory that argues the opposite, namely that individual meaning and social action is the foundation on which social structures are built.

In order to understand the rise of bureaucracy in modern society, then, Weber argued, we have to understand the meaning that individuals attribute to this kind of social structure. (Weber's theory of social action is also discussed in the context of interactionist theory in *What is Sociology?* (pages 46–7).)

Weber argued that there are three types of social action, 'emotional or affective action', 'traditional action', and 'rational action'.

Emotional or *affective action* refers to actions which are motivated or driven by emotion. This can refer to kindness shown to a person because of love or emotional attraction, but it can also refer to acts of violence stemming from a loss of temper.

Traditional action refers to actions motivated by custom. Customs are habits formed because 'things have always been done that way'. In this instance people just accept that things are done in a certain way without further question.

Rational action refers to an action with a very clear awareness of its specific goal. The actor carefully and systematically calculates the cost of attaining that goal, and hence decides on the most efficient way to reach that goal.

In Weber's understanding there are certain relationships in society based on inequality. Examples of this are a queen and her subjects, or a general and his soldiers. Sometimes people are forced to take subservient positions, but often they simply accept the authority of those with more power, material goods or prestige than themselves. The key word here is 'authority'. 'Authority' is different from 'power'. Power in Weberian terms implies the use of force, or the threat of using force, to get someone to do something that he or she does not want to do. In contrast, authority implies an acceptance of someone else's right to get you to do something.

But why do people accept the authority of a certain leader? Just as there are different motivations for social action, so authority is also derived from different sources. Weber directly draws on his notions of 'emotional or affective action', 'traditional action', and 'rational action' to explain why people accept the authority of others under certain conditions.

Furthermore, he uses his understanding of the different sources of authority to explain why people construct social organizations in certain ways. In other words, the acceptance of different forms of authority also leads to different organizational types. The table below shows the connections between particular kinds of social action, leadership and organization. You will see here how machine-like Weber's image is.

Fig 2.2: Connections between social action, leadership, and organization

	Pre-modern societies		Modern societies
Social action	Emotional/affective	Traditional	Rational
Authority	Charismatic	Traditional	Rational–legal
Organization	Religious sect	Patriarchal household	Bureaucracy

Charismatic authority, said Weber, refers to the acceptance of an individual's authority because of a call on emotion. The concept is derived from the term 'charisma', which indicates a capacity to inspire devotion and enthusiasm. The authority of the leader is accepted because of certain charismatic qualities. An example of such a leader might be Adolph Hitler. In the South African context, Eugene Terre'blanche, the right-wing Afrikaner leader, also attempts to construct authority amongst followers by appealing to emotion.

Since authority here usually depends on the personality of an individual, the forms of organization that emerge are fluid and sometimes short-lived. People are not appointed to positions because of their capability or even because they are related to the leader, but because they are loyal. When the leader is removed from the equation, the organization often collapses. Certain religious sects operate in this way. They rapidly gain popularity through the personality of a strong and colourful leader, and then fade quite fast when the leader dies or leaves the sect.

An ideal type, for Weber, is a mental model of the way various attributes of a phenomenon logically fit together although it does not exist in reality.

Traditional authority is derived from an appeal to custom and tradition. The role played by the patriarch in families in pre-industrial societies is an example of this. In the South African context, tribal chiefs derive their authority from custom. The forms of social organization that are constructed around traditional authority usually resemble patriarchal households, or communities formed around the interests of the leader. Organizational structures are maintained by custom, but these customs can change over time.

According to Weber, *rational–legal authority* becomes dominant in modern industrial societies, because an appeal to emotion and tradition is no longer effective. Emotion and tradition interfere with the requirement of efficiency. The costs of achieving certain goals can be calculated effectively only by suspending emotion and tradition.

The form of organization that supports rational action and rational–legal authority is the 'bureaucracy'. Weber argued that a process of bureaucratization would take place as industrial societies modernize, because no other kind of organization could handle the efficiency demands of modernity. Bureaucracy in its ideal type, said Weber, has certain important characteristics.

The characteristics of a bureaucracy comprise:

- *Division of labour*: In a bureaucracy, the organization's activities are broken down into specialized tasks, which become fixed duties. Individuals and departments are made responsible for the execution of those particular duties.
- *Hierarchy*: This refers to the chain of command in an organization, and the acceptance of responsibility of those in higher positions to supervise the actions of their subordinates.
- *Rules and regulations*: These lay down the responsibility and duties of those in positions of authority, as well as the procedures for the performance of regular tasks. Officials accept the authority of their superiors, because they believe that these rules are correct.
- *Professionalism*: The conduct of bureaucrats is governed by 'formalistic impersonality', not by personal feelings or emotion. Bureaucrats are motivated only by the rules and regulations of the bureaucracy.
- *Meritocracy*: Officials are appointed and promoted on the basis of their knowledge, skill, and proven technical expertise.
- *Separation of private and official income*: According to Weber, 'bureaucracy segregates official activity as something distinct from the sphere of private life'. Officials are not permitted to use any part of the organization for personal gain other than their remuneration.

Probably the best-known modern application of this machine metaphor in practice has been MacDonald's, the famous hamburger chain:

> *The firm has built a solid reputation for excellent performance in the fast-food industry by mechanizing the organization of all its franchise outlets all over the world so that each can produce a uniform product. It serves a carefully targeted mass market in a perfectly regular and consistent way, with all the precision that 'hamburger science' can provide* (Morgan 1997: 27).

For Weber bureaucracies were 'technically superior' to other kinds of organizations. They were infinitely more efficient. As a result, modern society would be increasingly dominated by soulless organizations of the bureaucratic kind.

The iron cage of bureaucracy

Weber further distinguishes between substantive rationality and formal rationality. Whereas *substantive rationality* implies a concern with 'the values and desired end of an action', *formal rationality* is 'concerned with calculable techniques and procedures'. In this light, Weber was very much aware of the problems presented by bureaucratic forms of organization. Bureaucracies in themselves create certain tendencies to undermine substantive rationality by focusing on formal rationality; in other words, they focus on technical procedures and rules rather than broader organizational aims.

Therefore, for example, bureaucrats tend to strengthen their own position within the organization by bolstering the position of their departments in opposition to other departments. This is the origin of the term 'bloated' bureaucracy. Also, officials may become caught up in 'red tape'. This is when the rules and regulations become so tedious to follow that, instead of being efficient, the organization gets bogged down in organizational inertia.

However, Weber argued, in capitalist societies capitalist bureaucracies would be disciplined by the market. When a business organization becomes inefficient, profits decrease. In some cases the organization goes bankrupt as a result. There will therefore be an incentive for business organizations to keep on rationalizing. This implies constant attention to whether organizational departments contribute to efficiency or not, and to rationalizing departments that do not contribute to efficiency.

For the state bureaucracy, on the other hand, there was, for Weber, the real danger that those in charge of it would not use such power to the advantage of society. It is therefore important to curtail the power of bureaucrats, especially those who control the state apparatus. This can be done by politicians who are democratically elected. They ensure that the bureaucracy is held accountable to citizens. Public scrutiny by democratic processes can bring secret deals between bureaucrats and powerful interests into the open.

The political scientist, Robert Michels, put it more strongly. He argued that bureaucracy inevitably produces a ruling elite which asserts its dominance by displacing organizational goals. This principle became known as the 'iron law of oligarchy'. (In chapter 3 we consider this theory more carefully in the context of the organizational transformation of trade unions in the South African context.)

In summary, Max Weber argued that industrialization would lead to a new dominant form of social organization, the bureaucracy. This is because rational forms of decision-making have a particular meaning for individuals. They link the achievement of goals to the efficient use of resources. As such they are technically superior to actions motivated by emotion or tradition. Bureaucratic forms of organization are more efficient at achieving certain goals than other organizational forms.

However, Weber was concerned about the fact that bureaucracy might become an 'iron cage' which limited people's freedom in modern societies. Hence the importance of the market and democratic political institutions as disciplining mechanisms.

In the history of social theory, Weber laid the sociological foundations for understanding large-scale organizations. But, as always in sociology, several thinkers engaged with this 'foundation' by questioning his assumptions about the nature of society and social organization.

Bureaucracy, efficiency, and control

A number of sociologists have questioned the extent to which bureaucratic work organization is inevitable. They argue that it is not always the most efficient form of work organization. Here we examine the work of three writers, Gouldner and Burawoy in the United States, and Phakati in South Africa.

In modern society bureaucracies are neither the most efficient nor the most common form of organization.

Alvin Gouldner did a study of a mine and a factory on the same premises. At the mine, gypsum was extracted, and then used as the major ingredient to manufacture wallboards in the other part of the factory. Work was organized in very different ways in the factory and in the mine (Gouldner 1954, 1972).

In the factory, there were important elements of a typical bureaucracy. Work procedures were standardized and there was a clear hierarchy in place. In the mine, however, workers had much more control over their work. Miners often rotated jobs and also repaired machinery themselves when it broke down. The hierarchy was less formal, and supervisors accepted the workers' own informal hierarchies. Gouldner also showed how miners successfully resisted attempts by a new manager to impose more bureaucratic work practices in the mine.

Gouldner makes a very important sociological point here. Some tasks are more suited to bureaucratization than others. In a factory, it is often possible to make work routine. Tasks are generally repetitive, and the product is standardized. However, in the mine conditions are more unpredictable. This requires more autonomy than allowed by bureaucratic models. Also, workers can actively resist attempts by the formal hierarchy to impose certain work procedures. These processes of conflict and compromise cannot be contained within just one organizational form. One should expect, then, argues Gouldner, that there will be differing degrees of bureaucratization.

This brings us to a key point made by Michael Burawoy in his study of an engineering factory in Chicago. In Burawoy's approach, bureaucracy is not necessarily about efficiency or rationality. Indeed, drawing on the approach developed in chapter 1 above, he argues that it is more about control. He had the benefit of a study that was done in the same factory 30 years earlier, and could compare his findings with those of the earlier study (Burawoy 1979).

He found, that over time, workers had achieved more autonomy over their work. In the earlier study, they were more closely supervised along the lines of scientific management. Burawoy described the strained relationship between workers and supervisors, and how workers had succeeded in doing their jobs, often *in spite of* supervision, rules, and regulations. Workers often bent rules in order to get their work done. He called this process 'making out'.

In the South African context, Sizwe Phakati showed that in gold mines there are disparities between the 'official' version of how work is supposed to take place and how work actually takes place underground. He argued that workers are often not supplied with sufficient materials to do the work they are supposed to do. Under these conditions, they apply a system they describe as 'planisa'. Roughly translated, this means 'to make a plan'. Without such an informal plan the work would not have been done at all (Phakati 2002).

In summary, whereas Weber saw bureaucracy as necessarily more efficient than other forms of work organization, subsequent sociological research shows how the demands of efficiency can require varying degrees of bureaucracy. This depends partly upon the extent to which workers resist bureaucratic control and hierarchy. The notions of 'making out' and 'planisa' show that there are limits to the extent to which rules and regulations enhance efficiency under unpredictable conditions. Often these same rules may prevent work from taking place and informal practices by workers outside the rules may actually enhance efficiency.

From bureaucracy to 'adhocracy'

Up to this point we have examined (quite critically) Weber's claim that the ideal-typical bureaucracy is the most efficient organization form. But Weber made a further claim flowing from this first one. He also argued that more and more organizations in industrial society would converge to resemble the ideal typical bureaucratic form. However, this view has also been challenged by sociologists and other social scientists. These critics of Weber argue that bureaucracies are too rigid, and that, far from converging into an ideal type of bureaucratic form, more flexible forms of organization are emerging.

Henry Mintzberg has argued that, contrary to Weber's one ideal-typical bureaucracy, business organizations could take on any one, or a combination, of five different forms of organization. He also argued that one of these forms, the 'adhocracy', would in the long run become the dominant form of organization (Mintzberg 1983).

Mintzberg, a management theorist, argued that in any business organization different groups of officials perform different functions. Over time, one of these groups tends to dominate the functioning of the organization, depending on what the organization is designed to achieve, and they put their stamp on the whole organization. Let us consider these groups and the organizations they create.

First, the *strategic apex* consists of top managers and corporate executives. They are responsible for the overall management of the business organization. The strategic apex usually forms the core of any new organization that has not yet developed a complex set of divisions. Mintzberg calls this kind of organizational structure a 'simple structure'.

Secondly, organizations usually have an *operating core*. This consists of workers who actually do production work, such as machine operators and assemblers in the case of a manufacturing concern. Organizations that are involved in standardized and routine work, such as manufacturing, are usually dominated by the 'operating core'. Mintzberg calls this kind of organization a 'machine bureaucracy'. This is close to Weber's ideal-typical bureaucracy.

Thirdly, the *technostructure* is responsible for designing and standardizing the work processes of the operating core. People involved in strategic planning, the training of staff, or the scheduling of production are part of the technostructure. An organization that is dominated by its technostructure is called a 'professional bureaucracy'. Professional bureaucracies also operate in stable environments where routine work is done, but in contrast to the machine bureaucracy, the work is done by professionally trained staff, such as teachers, accountants, or doctors, who have more autonomy in their work than in the machine bureaucracy.

Fourthly, the *middle line* consists of middle management and supervisors. They are the link between the strategic apex and the operating core. Very large organizations tend to be dominated by the middle line, especially multi-national corporations that have divisions in different countries. Mintzberg calls this the 'divisionalized form' of organization.

Fifthly, an organization's *support staff* are the professionals who are not directly involved in production or the servicing of clients. They provide support to the actual organization. They may be industrial relations officials, research and development staff, or payroll administrators. Organizations that are dominated by support staff actually depart substantially from Weber's notion of bureaucracy. These kinds of organization are very fluid, and they operate on the basis of teams of individuals who are brought together to work on projects. These teams are usually coordinated by support staff, and may include a number of specialized professionals and people with more generic skills. These teams do not have standardized procedures, and are usually dissolved once a certain problem is solved, hence the relevance of the term 'ad hoc'.

Fig 2.3: Mintzberg's organizational types

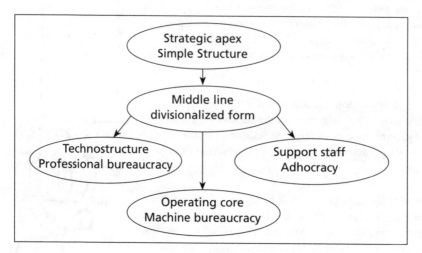

Mintzberg argued that when organizational environments require flexibility and innovation, the 'adhocracy' would be the best organizational form. Most new industries – such as the information technology (IT), advertising, consulting, and research industries – require this approach. For this reason, the 'adhocracy' would slowly become the dominant form of organizational structure. However, routine tasks would still require machine bureaucracies and professional bureaucracies (*see also* Haralambos & Holborn 1995: 281–4). What kind of image of an organization is Mintzberg presenting here? Morgan argues that this is a more sophisticated organic metaphor. It proposes that organizations can and do respond quite sensitively to their surrounding environments. Some kinds of technology and production demand one kind of organization, say machine bureaucracies; other kinds of technology and production demand other kinds of organization, say 'adhocracies'.

There is here a close and detailed relationship between organizations and their environments – much like the evolutionary relationship proposed by Charles Darwin (Morgan 1977: 44–71).

From Fordist to post-Fordist and network organizations

In chapter 1 we argued that from the 1970s onwards there was a transition from Fordist to post-Fordist forms of production. Whereas Fordist production was based on assembly-line production, machinery designed for repetitive tasks, mass output, and deskilling, post-Fordism is based on teamwork, multi-skilled workers, general-purpose machinery, batch production, and just-in-time delivery. It is easy to see that a post-Fordist approach to production leads to substantial flexibility in the organization, and that bureaucratic design principles are no longer appropriate.

Manuel Castells makes the same point when he argues that a whole new phase, that of global informational capitalism, is emerging. According to Castells, the 'network' is increasingly taking over as an organizational principle from the 'bureaucracy'. Where bureaucracies are rigid, networks are flexible. They change constantly, and transform notions of time and space in the process. (Remember our discussion of networks in chapter 1.)

Post-Fordism is not necessarily labour-friendly at all.

Some who profess the end of bureaucracy, notably post-Fordists, also argue that these new forms of work organization may lead to the empowerment of individuals in a post-bureaucratic organizational context. The following table counterpoises some of what are 'old' (the bureaucratic) and what are 'new' (the post-bureaucratic) characteristics.

Fig 2.4: Towards post-bureaucratic organizations?

Old	New
stability	disorganization/chaos
rationality	charisma/values
planning	spontaneity
control	empowerment
command	participation
centralization	decentralization/disaggregation
hierarchy	network
formal	informal/flexibility
large	downsized/de-layered

Source: Thompson & McHugh (1995: 167).

The above table contrasts 'control', 'planning' and 'command' in bureaucratic organizations with 'empowerment', 'spontaneity' and 'participation' in post-bureaucratic organizations. In a way, this perspective argues, post-bureaucratic organizations can move us beyond the 'iron cage' of bureaucracy.

This kind of argument is also made in the South Africa context. The most prominent example is the Industrial Strategy Project (ISP), a team of researchers commissioned by COSATU to investigate productivity in the South African manufacturing industry in the early 1990s. However, as we shall see, they came to a problematic conclusion (Joffe, Kaplan, Kaplinsky, & Lewis 1995).

South African manufacturing firms during the apartheid era were unproductive, the researchers argued, because they were protected from competition by high import tariffs. As a result, they failed to shift their Fordist approach to a post-Fordist one. Fordism in South Africa, along with racist managerial practices, they said, led to distrust in the workplace. If managers adopted post-Fordist techniques such as quality circles, teamwork, suggestion schemes, and multi-skilling, they could transform South African factories into high-wage and high-productivity workplaces. Post-Fordism, said the ISP, was a 'labour-friendly' approach to flexible production, and an effective way to address the legacy of apartheid in the workplace.

Yet there is a problem with this approach. Several studies have shown that so-called flexible approaches to managing organizations are not always that 'labour friendly'. As indicated in chapter 1, globalization has increased competition between firms. It has also opened up the threat that firms will relocate to countries where labour is more docile and cheaper. Indeed, Castells argues that capital and labour now operate in two different spatial realms and do not relate to each other as they did in the past. Production facilities no longer form part of production conglomerates, but part of networks. They can be included and excluded from production by subcontracting and other arm's-length type contractual relationships. This substantially decreases the power of workers to negotiate (Castells 1996).

To summarize, a significant number of writers argue that the dominance of ideal-typical bureaucratic organizations has ended, or is coming to an end. While some of them may work with different theoretical frameworks, they have in common the view that there is a trend away from bureaucratic organization towards 'adhocratic', post-Fordist, or network organizations. Some argue that new post-bureaucratic forms of work organization would lead to the empowerment of workers. However, others dispute these claims by arguing that this 'flexibility' leads to new forms or organizational domination and exploitation – what some call 'flexploitation'.

Conclusion

Organizations can be seen, then, from a number of different perspectives. As always in sociology, theory progresses by argument and counter-argument, by counterposing one image or metaphor against another. In this chapter we have seen how system theorists/functionalists view organizations as a pattern of interrelated subsystems. They use the metaphor of an organism. But like functionalists in other areas of sociology, they have been criticized by Marxist-inclined critical theorists.

For critical theorists, organizations are not detached or insulated from society. In fact, they are embedded in broader social relations. Also, it is important to study organizations in all their multi-faceted dimensions. Organizations are not always orderly entities based on 'value consensus'. As we argued in chapter 1, the social organization of work is very often contested, and attempts to control and contain this contestation lead to new forms of control. This, in turn, opens up new possibilities for contestation. Critical theorists then often use the image of an organization as an instrument of control by the ruling class.

We also pointed out that for Max Weber bureaucracy is the organizational form for rational action in industrial society. For Weber, the ideal-typical bureaucracy was like a smooth-running machine. Whereas Weber thought bureaucratic forms of organization would be more efficient than other forms, he was concerned about the extent to which bureaucracy could limit freedom.

We then showed that bureaucracy is not always the most effective way of organizing work, especially when the organization operates in an unpredictable environment. Often, the informal actions of workers contribute to organizational efficiency outside the formal rules and regulations of the organization. Also, workers often resist the imposition of bureaucratic structures when these lead to a curtailment of their organizational autonomy. It follows that, when one studies organizations, it is important to examine both their formal and their informal dynamics. One also has to take into account that organizations are not unitary, harmonious entities, but that their orders are often fiercely contested.

A number of theorists also argue that bureaucracy as an organizational form is declining, since more flexible forms or organization, such as 'adhocracy', post-Fordism, or the network organization are taking its place. However, there is disagreement as to whether these new organizational forms would lead to a more empowering workplace.

Building on our understanding of the different phases of work organization in chapter 1 and the perspective developed in this chapter, we can historically contextualize the development of different organizational forms over time in the diagram below.

Fig 2.5: The development of organizational forms over time

Historical period	Form of organization
Rise of the factory	Simple forms of organization and direct control by entrepreneurs
Rise of scientific management	Beginnings of bureaucracy by 'rationalization', standardization of work procedures, and specialized supervisors
Rise of Fordism	Large-scale bureaucratic organizations
Rise of post-Fordism	Hybrid organizational forms, including the 'flexible firm', network organizations, 'adhocracy', and post-Fordist organizations

In this chapter we have considered various ways of understanding organizations, by examining various theories and the metaphors that they work with. In the next chapter, we analyse trade unions as contradictory organizations, because they are both professional bureaucracies and social movements dedicated to challenging unequal power relationships in society.

3 Trade Unions as Movements and Organizations

As elsewhere in the world, South African trade unions are a curious mixture of politicized social movement and more formal organization. In the transition to democracy since 1994, they have lost a significant amount of their power and influence.

Introduction

Trade unions arose historically as an attempt by workers to counteract employers' power.

Chapters 1 and 2 have focused on the related themes of work, bureaucracy, and organizations. The focus of this chapter is on trade unions and their role as a counter-force to managerial control and bureaucracy in the workplace. The discussion examines the tension inherent in trade unionism between the desire to mobilize and contest for power, on the one hand, and pressures to achieve efficiency through formal and permanent organizational structures, on the other. Finally the discussion provides a brief historical sketch of trade unions in South Africa and highlights some of the key changes taking place in contemporary South African trade unionism.

Trade unions are organizations formed by workers in the workplace to advance their collective interests in an environment dominated by employers. The history of trade unionism is linked to the transformation of work and the development of modern industrial society. The emergence and growth of trade unions is an indication of the contradictions inherent in capitalism: the owners of capital employ workers to produce goods and services and in return pay them a wage; but while it is in the interests of both parties for the relationship to continue, their *interests remain contradictory*. On the one hand, employers want to increase their profit by controlling workers and keeping the cost of labour low; on the other hand, workers want to increase their wages. Thus, what is a gain for the employer by way of high profits is a loss to the worker. Similarly, high wages for workers can be achieved only by reducing employers' profits.

The context within which trade unions emerge is very important for this discussion. Both at the level of the workplace and in society as a whole, relations between workers and employers are characterized by the *inequality of power relations*. This means that an individual worker is less powerful in relation to his or her employer and, likewise, workers as a class have less power than the class of employers in society. It is this weakness of the individual worker which gives rise to the desire by workers to combine together in a collective body called a 'trade union'. The primary reason for combination is the desire to build solidarity around common interests with the aim of reducing the inequality of power relations. Thus a union plays a central role in the regulation of workplace relations and in contesting the power of employers to control production. As we will show in the discussion on social movement unionism later in this chapter, some unions can play a similar role beyond the shop floor.

Origins and brief history of trade unions

The origins of trade unions can be traced back to late eighteenth-century England when groups of craftsmen in several trades or occupations formed craft or trade unions. The main aims of combining in unions were to fight for better wages, to ensure job control, and to prevent the dilution of their skills. (Remember our discussion in chapter 1.) Since those early years, the development of trade unionism has been linked to patterns of industrialization in different societies and to contradictions within the capitalist system. In particular, the evolution of trade unionism has been linked to the transformation of the labour process over the last two and a half centuries. Thus the shift from craft to industrial unionism is linked to the transition from small-scale and craft production to the mass production of goods using Fordist methods in the twentieth century.

From England ideas about trade unionism spread to other parts of the world, including British territories overseas. Emigrant workers who had experienced trade unionism in England took these ideas with them and became pioneers of new union movements in their new countries, including South Africa. In South Africa during the last quarter of the nineteenth century, these workers were concentrated in certain sectors of the economy such as printing, plumbing, and mining.

But despite these early beginnings, South African workers remained divided along racial lines and these divisions were reproduced at the level of union organization. They emerged and were reproduced by different groups for several reasons. At the heart of the divisions were the colour bars – the wage colour bar and the job colour bar (Johnstone 1994). According to Johnstone, the *wage colour bar* was a set of 'racially discriminatory controls which operated to secure and perpetuate the cheapness of African labour' (1994: 129). Under this system African workers were paid lower wages than white workers, and these mechanisms were both instituted and maintained by employers. The wage colour bar sought to ensure the cheapness of African labour by limiting competition among employers for African labour and by putting in place measures to create a servile labour force. Mining, particularly gold, was the most successful industry in implementing this system.

The *job colour bar*, in contrast, was a system of systematic occupational and racial discrimination against black workers instituted by different industries at the insistence of white workers and their unions. Under this system, black workers were barred from certain jobs and occupations and were thus relegated to unskilled jobs in the labour market. Although the state played an ambiguous role in creating and reproducing these divisions, it nevertheless supported them by passing the Industrial Conciliation Act 11 of 1924, which specifically excluded black workers from the statutory definition of an employee. This law created a dual system in which white workers became insiders and black workers outsiders to the industrial relations system. To all intents and purposes, white trade unions supported the apartheid system and ceased to perform the classical function of a trade union, namely, a class organization.

Meanwhile, black trade unions emerged for the first time at the end of the World War I. The first black union organization was the Industrial and Commercial Workers' Union which at the height of its popularity in the mid-1920s had about 100 000 members. But for many decades black unions went through cycles of mobilization, growth, suppression, and collapse. Their failure to consolidate their growth and ensure permanent organization was due to four key factors, namely:

- an inability to gain recognition from employers;
- repression by the state;
- opposition by white unions, and
- inappropriate choice of strategies by leadership.

However, the revival of black trade unionism in the early 1970s marked the beginning of a new cycle which differed from the familiar pattern. Not only were the new unions able to mobilize and grow; they also succeeded in establishing permanent organizational structures. The examples used in the rest of this chapter are drawn from this tradition of trade unionism as it provides a richness of material for sociological analysis that none of the other cycles and traditions provides. These unions have been in existence for almost 30 years now and have gone through all the phases of mobilization, growth, and consolidation. So let us now consider the theoretical issues raised by the rise of these trade unions.

The role of trade unions in regulating workplace relations

Trade unions can play either defensive or more transformative roles.

At a simple descriptive level we can say that the functions of a trade union are to *struggle for better wages and improved conditions* of work for their members. These functions can be broken down further to include such things as negotiating for better wages, fighting for better and fair grading of jobs, ensuring that workers get paid for skills they possess, ensuring a healthy and safe work environment, taking up workers' grievances, and defending workers in disciplinary hearings.

But sociologists would conceptualize the role of trade unions as one which seeks to *regulate workplace relations* in a manner that is beneficial to its members. Such efforts go beyond merely struggling for better wages and conditions and often entail *contestation for power*. Thus the notion of regulating workplace relations refers not only to the defensive dimension of union struggles but also to its radical one. A union's struggle is defensive if its aim is to maintain existing rights and secure modest adjustments to wages and conditions. A radical struggle, on the other hand, is one that aims at achieving significant changes not only in relation to wages and conditions but also in relation to altering the balance of power in favour of workers. Of course, in real life the distinction between defensive and radical struggles is not so clear cut.

The role of unions in regulating workplace relations can be illustrated by referring to the struggles of the black unions which emerged after 1973. When these unions started organizing in the early 1970s, workplace relations were characterized by the existence of racially despotic forms of managerial control or what Webster (1985) has referred to as *racial despotism*. 'Racial despotism' refers to a system of managerial control that relies on coercion rather than consent and in which black employees are subordinated to white employees. Von Holdt (2000) has termed this form of control the *apartheid workplace regime*. In the early years of union organization most worker struggles were defensive in nature and their chances of mounting a successful challenge to racial despotism appeared remote. However, by the end of the 1980s there were clear signs that most workplaces were shifting to new and moderate forms of workplace control. These shifts were the outcome of two main factors. One was successful mobilization by workers and their unions. The second was the legislation flowing from the report of the Wiehahn Commission in 1979, instituted by a more reformist government.

During the 1970s and 1980s trade unions underwent dramatic changes.

Workplace relations in the 1990s and the early 2000s were marked by significant concessions made by management (and the state) to workers. Among these were:

- A new dispensation of rights. For example, a worker now has a right to belong (or not to belong) to a union.
- New procedures for processing worker grievances and defending individual rights. For example, every worker now has a right to a fair and procedural disciplinary hearing before disciplinary action is taken against him or her.
- Acceptance of the principle of equity in the workplace. This includes equity in relation to appointment, training, promotion, and remuneration.

It must be noted, however, that a union's ability to regulate workplace relations successfully does not depend solely on its ability to mobilize and contest. It is also dependent on the strategic location of union members in the labour process. If union members have highly specialized skills or if they are strategically located in the production process, the union stands a better chance of influencing change in the workplace. On the contrary, if a union's members are located in unskilled and other vulnerable positions in the production process, their ability to influence change is reduced. Furthermore, changes in the way work is done may weaken a trade union's ability to influence or regulate workplace relations. In chapter 1 we discussed new forms of work under globalization such as outsourcing, casualization, and growing informalization of·work. These new forms of work undermine the ability of unions to have a strong voice in the workplace.

At this point we must add that just as the labour process is subject to change and transformation, so are trade unions as collective bodies of workers. This can also reduce the power of these bodies to regulate workplace relations. Let us now discuss unions as organizations and as movements.

Trade unions as organizations and movements

Theorists of social change and collective behaviour agree that change in society does not just happen. Social change occurs because of collective action by groups of people who have common interests and share a common desire to change the existing social order. Unorganized groups of people at times embark on *informal* or *covert forms of resistance* to express their dissatisfaction with the authorities. But as a collective consciousness develops people often embark on collective action that takes the form of *formal* or *overt resistance* (Cohen 1994).

A *social movement* is a coordinated attempt by a group of people to achieve a common goal. Whereas the goals of some movements are directed at reforming the existing social order, many other movements aim to implement an alternative vision of society. A movement is characterized by an informality of organization and a weakness or absence of hierarchical structures. The methods that a social movement adopts to achieve its goals are often radical and involve agitation, mobilization, and contestation. While some of these methods may be legal, others may be unconventional and even illegal. In their early stages most forms of organized collective action take on the character of a social movement.

By contrast, a *formal organization* is characterized by formality, structure, and hierarchy. Formal organizations generally operate within the parameters set by the authorities and the law. Thus, instead of mobilization and contestation, an organization follows established channels, procedures, and laws to achieve its goals and secure the interests of its members.

Of course, this distinction does not always operate so neatly in practice. In other words, these concepts are mere *ideal types*. In real life there is a considerable degree of overlap between a movement and an organization. A trade union illustrates this overlap. On the one hand, a trade union is a social movement in that it relies on contestation and mobilization to achieve its goals. The fact that it is engaged in a power struggle with employers means that it cannot rely solely on established procedures and laws to win gains for its members. After all, these procedures and laws are often established through the influence of employers. On the other hand, a trade union has the characteristics of a formal organization in that, for it to function effectively and efficiently, it has to establish a certain degree of formality, structure, and hierarchy. In short, a trade union involves a tension between mobilization and contestation, on the one hand, and structure and formality, on the other.

This tension means that a trade union has some social movement elements within it, while at the same time being an organization. But a new union that is small and struggling to survive and get employer and state recognition is more likely to display stronger characteristics of a movement. On the contrary, a large union which has achieved recognition by the authorities is more likely to function like a typical organization as discussed above. Thus, during its life a trade union often changes from being more of a social movement to being more of an organization, and back again. Indeed, some have used the term 'movement organization' to capture this tension within a trade union.

The social and political role of trade unions

Up to this point we have been discussing trade unions only in relation to the workplace. But unions in many countries have played an active role in struggles beyond the workplace. An example of this is the role played by South African unions in the struggle for democracy. These unions formed alliances with liberation movements and other organizations in civil society to mobilize around issues which affected their members and their communities. Webster has called this approach *social movement unionism* in that the unions have two faces. The economic dimension of the union is about trying to achieve increases and improvements in wages and conditions. The other, the political dimension, is about acting as a voice for its members on social and political issues (Webster 1994).

Social movement unionism requires that a union should be able to mobilize its members and get them to participate in union affairs and the running of campaigns. Thus, this kind of unionism is about building the union movement into a powerful counter-force which sees a connection between workers' problems in the workplace and those that they face in the broader society.

Oligarchic tendencies in trade unions

The sociological study of trade unions draws insights from the sociological study of organizations, particularly the work of Weber and Michels. The main concern of these theorists was 'the tendency for organizations to develop a life of their own, apart from the membership which created them' (Crouch 1982: 162). In other words, although an organization is created by individual members, it tends to become more than the sum total of those members' wishes. It becomes a social entity or institution in its own right, with its own patterns of power and control.

Michels thought that all organizations tend to become dominated by a small leadership group.

The work of Michels on the emergence of oligarchic tendencies in political parties and trade unions has been influential throughout the twentieth century. His ideas influenced many theorists who belong to what has been termed the *pessimistic tradition* in the study of trade unionism. These theorists argue that democracy in trade unions is unsustainable and that this limits the ability of these bodies to champion democratic change in society.

Michels argued that, beyond a certain size, organizations cannot exist without an impersonal bureaucracy. They need complex financial, legal, and organizational expertise which becomes difficult for the rank and file to control. They also need leaders who, over time, tend to fight for the maintenance of their own power rather than for the goals of the organization. There is, therefore, said Michels, an inherent conflict between democracy and organization, and an irresistible trend for large organizations to become dominated by small groups of powerful individuals, hence his term, the *iron law of oligarchy*.

In his study of American unionism Richard Lester arrived at a similar conclusion, namely, that these unions had experienced certain internal changes since the 1930s. The main trend which he noted was that many of them had been 'shedding their youthful characteristics in the process of settling down or "maturing"' (Lester 1958: 21). Unions tend to go through a 'natural evolution of organizational life' characterized by stages of development which began with a radical and democratic stage. But once organizations gain recognition by employers and society as a whole, a transformation occurs in terms of organizational goals, the nature of leadership, internal operations, and the distribution of power and functions among its different structural levels. These changes are invariably accompanied by the emergence of a hierarchy and an oligarchy, the shifting of some functions and decisions from local to higher levels, and the development of impersonal relations between top officials and the rank-and-file membership.

The *optimistic tradition*, in contrast, is often associated with the early work of Karl Marx and Friedrich Engels and their treatment of trade union struggles. Although they were mindful of the limitations of trade unions in the face of a powerful bourgeois class, they saw the importance of trade unions as being a political consciousness-building one. As Engels wrote in the 1840s:

> *That these Unions contribute to nourish the bitter hatred of the workers against the property-holding class need hardly be said. ... Strikes ... are the military school of the working-men in which they prepare themselves for the great struggle which cannot be avoided; they are the* pronunciamentos *of single branches of industry that these too have joined the labour movement ... And as schools of war, the Unions are unexcelled* (Engels 1973: 226–31).

Therefore, for Marx and Engels, trade unions were the first step in the emergence of a revolutionary class consciousness which would later result in a direct challenge to the capitalist system.

However, in later years these authors were disappointed by the lack of revolutionary activity in trade union ranks. They gave three explanations for this, namely:

- a minority of privileged workers were able to get concessions from the bosses;
- corruption of union leaders occurred, made possible by the apathy of the rank and file, and
- the rise of *embourgeoisement* among the British working class. *Embourgeoisement* means that a working class's standard of living improves to such an extent that many in this class adopt or aspire to a bourgeois lifestyle.

According to John Kelly, this ambivalence in Marx and Engels' work on trade unions was related to swings between periods of high militancy and mobilization and those of quiescence by the working class. Thus, it was during periods of quiescence resulting from economic growth (such as the 1850s and the early 1860s) and economic stagnation (such as that in the late 1870s and early 1880s) that the two 'gave vent to their deepest reservations and their most hostile judgements on the emerging trade unions with their fondness for "bourgeois respectability"' (Kelly 1988: 11–12).

Since the end of the World War II a number of studies have been undertaken to test the proposition of oligarchy in trade unions. Many of these have emphasized the existence of countervailing factors which discourage oligarchic tendencies (for example, Lipset, Trow, & Coleman 1956; Hyman 1971). Although these studies acknowledge the contribution of the pessimists, particularly Michels, they challenge the existence of an 'iron law'. Hyman argues that, although oligarchic tendencies exist in trade unions, there are also *countervailing forces* which discourage oligarchy.

A recent study which makes an important contribution to the debates is that by Voss and Sherman (2000). These scholars argue that a revitalization and radicalization of goals and tactics can occur within highly oligarchic and conservative organizations. Their study of American unions shows that this radicalization occurred in some unions following the entry of activists with previous experience of activism and the intervention of national union leadership to empower local structures.

Let us now turn to a discussion of recent developments within the South African trade union movement. In this discussion we note that unions in South Africa have changed and we consider the reasons why this has happened. We also examine the nature of the changes they have undergone.

Why and how have South African trade unions changed?

Webster and Adler (1999) propose that South Africa is going through a 'double transition'. It is a double transition because, on the one hand, the country is moving politically from authoritarianism to democracy and, on the other, it is moving from an economy of international isolation and inward-looking industrialization to one which is open to global influence.

Trade unions were central actors in the democratization process.

These processes present unions with greater opportunities for enhancing their influence in society, particularly with regard to shaping the unfolding processes of change. On the other hand, democratization and globalization have imposed new constraints and challenges for trade unions which threaten to diminish their power and cancel their influence. This dilemma shows the ironic relationship of unions to processes of democratic change. While they are often central players in bringing about democratic change, they can find themselves shunted off the centre stage as soon as the transition has occurred.

South African unions played a key role in the struggle for democracy in the 1980s and early 1990s. This made them central actors in the democratization process. First, they found themselves playing the role of power broker, with the major political parties vying for their support. COSATU entered into an alliance with the ANC and the SACP. This alliance ensured it a central role in the transition and afforded it an opportunity to influence the policies of the new government. In particular, COSATU's proposal for a social democratic Reconstruction and Development Programme (RDP), which put emphasis on redistribution rather than the market, was later adopted by the ANC as its policy and election platform in the run-up to the 1994 elections.

Secondly, a number of unions and federations took advantage of their association with some political parties to get some of their key leaders to stand for parliament in the 1994 elections. COSATU released 20 of its top leaders, including its then general secretary, Jay Naidoo, to stand for parliament on an ANC ticket. Some of these leaders later became influential members of the new ANC-led government.

Thirdly, one of the areas in which unions have made tangible gains is policy formulation. The unions have been involved in shaping government policies, particularly those to do with the labour market. The new Labour Relations Act 66 of 1995 (LRA) is the centrepiece of these progressive labour-friendly reforms. Adopted in 1995 after thorough consultation with unions and business, the Act codifies organizational rights for workers and trade unions, introduces simple and more accessible dispute-resolution procedures, extends coverage to virtually all workers, entrenches the right to strike, and puts in place building blocks for workplace democratization. Other labour-friendly reforms include the Basic Conditions of Employment Act 75 of 1997, the Employment Equity Act 55 of 1998, and the Skills Development Act 89 of 1999.

Finally, the creation of new institutions has opened a new area of opportunities for the union movement. Chief among these institutions is the corporatist National Economic Development and Labour Council (Nedlac), where labour, together with government and business, is a central player, together in the formulation of labour market and macro-economic policy. All major policy and legislative proposals have to be presented and discussed at Nedlac before they are debated in parliament, a process which affords unions an opportunity to shape policy at an early stage.

In a nutshell, democratization has opened new avenues for the union movement to exercise a tremendous amount of influence in the reshaping of South African society and the spectrum of issues over which the movement has influence is much wider than that available to unions in countries of a similar level of development as South Africa.

However, the advent of democracy and globalization has introduced new constraints and threats for unions. The September Commission, an investigative team appointed by COSATU in 1996 to explore strategies for organizational renewal, noted in its final report that unions run the risk of becoming victims of the very transition they fought for. The following section highlights some of the weaknesses facing the union movement. Many of these are drawn from the report of the September Commission and the work of Buhlungu (2001).

Demobilization and weak structures

South Africa's transition to democracy has been accompanied by declining enthusiasm of the rank and file in all social movements, including the trade unions. A 1996 COSATU discussion document lamented 'the demobilization of our people' and observed that 'most activists are no more sure of what the strategic objectives are'. This confusion has been accompanied by a visible weakening of organizational structures and the decline of grassroots creativity and leadership. The September Commission (1997) considered the following factors in their analyses.

Trade unions in the new South Africa have lost much of the influence and power they had.

The brain drain

Since 1994 hundreds of experienced unionists have left the movement in search of greener pastures elsewhere. This 'brain drain' includes rank-and-file activists, shop stewards, branch, regional and national worker leaders, and full-time officials, including administrators, organizers, regional secretaries, and general secretaries. A survey of COSATU full-time officials conducted in 1996–1997 revealed that the majority of officials (57 per cent) had not completed four years in the unions at the time they were surveyed and that only 24 per cent of officials were in the unions in the 1970s and 1980s.

The brain drain is a direct consequence of the deracialization of society and the consequent opening up of new opportunities for upward mobility for skilled black people. The majority of ex-unionists have moved into politics, local government, the civil service, state corporations, the private sector (as personnel or human resource officers or managers), union investment companies, and some non-governmental organizations (NGOs) (Buhlungu 2001).

Lack of organizational capacity

The changing political and economic environment has forced the unions to confront new realities and challenges. Most have shown themselves incapable of sustaining their influence in some of the new institutions such as Nedlac. They tend to operate in an *ad hoc*, reactive, and inefficient way, or what the September Commission termed 'zigzag unionism'.

This lack of capacity is particularly glaring in the face of work restructuring by management. Strategies and tactics which helped the unions develop their power and influence under apartheid do not necessarily produce the same positive results in an era where capital is more mobile (Buhlungu 2001).

Vanishing utopias

The glue that held the union movement together in the past was a clear sense of purpose, political objectives, and a common value system. However, with the end of apartheid, it is no longer obvious to all who the enemy is. COSATU is in alliance with the ruling party and even those federations and unions which are not have maintained cordial relations with the new government. Many unionists have accepted the notion of 'social partnership' between labour, capital, and the state and there has been a degree of *rapprochement* between capital and labour, particularly at the top (Buhlungu 2001).

Therefore, today there is a pervasive sense of political confusion regarding the future of the workers' struggle. While many unions claim to be opposed to capitalism in favour of socialism, virtually all the post-1973 unions and federations (NACTU and COSATU) have established investment companies which are buying shares in some of the major corporations in the name of 'black economic empowerment'. Related to this is the fact that, although the unions have a well-known position against privatization and outsourcing, the investment companies of some of these unions are often among the top bidders when state corporations are up for sale. These trends are accompanied by the disappearance of idealism and utopian notions of a radical transformation of society since the collapse of existing socialism in Eastern Europe. Today, socialist rhetoric is merely an article of faith that has little or no relation to union practice.

Erosion of union traditions

For many years some in the union movement assumed that the militancy of the workers and the democratic traditions of the movement would endure into the future. However, there has been a considerable erosion of some of the practices and traditions. This is bringing about a new orientation to the values and politics of the unions in a way which bears some similarities to what has been observed in established movements elsewhere in the world.

This erosion of the tradition of grassroots unionism known as worker control has resulted in competition for power and material benefits that higher leadership positions carry. In some cases such competition has led to in-fighting and a debilitating fragmentation in unions (Buhlungu 2001).

There is a generational change at leadership levels and the consciousness of the new generation of leaders and activists is resulting in a significant shift of power from workers and constitutional structures to full-time officials. This shift is manifested in diminishing leadership accountability to the rank and file and goal displacement, as Michels would have predicted.

The creation of new collective bargaining and national-level institutions such as industry bargaining councils and Nedlac is resulting in a centralization of power and decision-making in the hands of leaders who are not accountable to the rank and file. This is leaving lower-level union structures such as shop stewards' committees and local shop stewards' councils in a state of powerlessness.

Class formation and realignment

Liberation and the deracialization of society have resulted in accelerated processes of class formation as some black people are catapulted into positions of power, wealth, and privilege. Old values, loyalties, and bonds of solidarity built during the years of mass mobilization have disintegrated, and notions of sacrifice and the collective ethic of the struggle days have been replaced by individualism and a quest for personal wealth accumulation.

COSATU has lost dozens of its leaders to government and the private sector.

Unionists who believe that unions offer limited opportunities for upward mobility and 'uncompetitive' remuneration packages have joined the ranks of the new elite and, already, ambitious unionists have been rewarded handsomely. Ex-unionists who have achieved instant success in business include

Cyril Ramaphosa, former general secretary of NUM, Marcel Golding, ex-deputy general secretary of NUM, and Johnny Copelyn, ex-general secretary of the South African Clothing and Textile Workers' Union (SACTWU). Ramaphosa left his union in 1991 to become the secretary general of the ANC. In 1994 he became an ANC member of parliament but left politics in 1997 to take advantage of new opportunities in the world of business. Golding and Copelyn were part of the group of 20 unionists released by COSATU in 1994 to go to parliament as ANC MPs. After a short stint in parliament they went into business and then rode the wave of so-called 'black economic empowerment'. Today all three are multi-millionaires (Buhlungu 2001).

A patronage relationship between the ANC and COSATU unions has emerged in which loyalty to the ANC/COSATU/SACP alliance is rewarded by appointment to legislative structures or the civil service. Hundreds of unionists have been rewarded in this way. In the 1999 elections key COSATU leaders, including four of the six national office-bearers (president, first vice-president, general secretary, and national treasurer), went to provincial legislatures and parliament. COSATU's former general secretary, Mbhazima Sam Shilowa, was appointed by the ANC as the premier of Gauteng Province, the economic powerhouse of South Africa. These appointments are not confined to the top. In 1994 and 1995 scores of regional and local unionists (organizers, shop stewards, and worker activists) were included in electoral lists and subsequently became municipal councillors, mayors, members of provincial legislatures, or members of provincial executive councils. Other unionists have moved into business.

However, it is not necessarily the act of going into politics or business which defines these ex-unionists as members of the new elite. It is the fact that their new jobs enable them to inherit all the trappings of power and privilege, including inflated salaries and perks, which were previously reserved for the elite under apartheid. Thus, in the context of a pervasive quest for personal wealth accumulation, for many unionism has become a launch pad for a successful career in politics, business, or the civil service.

The impact of globalization on unions

In addition to the above processes, globalization has introduced other constraints for South African unions. It has changed the balance of power in favour of capital. In the late 1980s the union movement had the initiative and was able to dictate the pace and direction of change through the use of mass action, resulting in a modification of some of the crude aspects of racial despotism and exploitation. However, globalization has enabled capital to seize the initiative and put the unions on the defensive. Although the unions are still able to mobilize and take action, such mobilization and action are defensive strategies in a context at which workers are faced with unemployment and retrenchment.

First, globalization has facilitated capital mobility from one country to another and from one region of the world to another. In recent years many South African companies have been investing in other countries on the African continent, where labour markets are perceived to be more flexible. Similarly, foreign companies have the option of moving to cheaper labour zones across the world. This mobility has drastically limited the options of labour in dealing with capital.

Secondly, the restructuring of work and the introduction of more flexible forms of work such as subcontracting and homework threaten the very existence of trade unions. It is much more difficult to organize workers under these fragmented conditions. Sectors of the economy which have been hit hardest by work restructuring and the introduction of flexible forms of work include retail, mining, and clothing and textiles.

Thirdly, globalization threatens to erode labour rights. Although South Africa has a new labour dispensation which grants these rights and protections, business has mounted a frontal attack on these new protections. The South African Foundation (SAF), a lobby group representing powerful business interests, is leading the charge against what they consider to be an extremely inflexible labour market. What they propose is a two-tier labour market, with the one tier enjoying labour rights while the second 'free entry' tier will be exempted from labour rights and minimum standards. Notions of economic liberalization such as these have significant support within the ANC.

Finally, the new ANC Government has been shifting gradually to the right since it assumed office in 1994 and this shift is characterized by an acceptance of the logic of neo-liberal globalization. (Neo-liberalism indicates a 'free market' state economic policy which promotes openness to globalization and a withdrawal of government from intervention in the market.) The first indications of this shift were the adoption of a neo-liberal macro-economic policy known as the Growth, Employment and Redistribution (GEAR) and the decision to privatize state corporations. This was followed by a downgrading of the RDP, and the demotion of ex-unionist Jay Naidoo, who was a minister responsible for implementing the programme. Meanwhile, the ANC Government has developed a very cosy relationship with the World Bank and the International Monetary Fund (IMF) (Buhlungu,2001).

The table below provides a schematic summary of the above changes both in the environment within which unions operate and within the unions themselves.

We must make a few points of caution about figure 3.1 on the next page. The year 1994 is used as an important year to indicate when most of these changes became visible. But in reality some of the changes emerged long before 1994. Furthermore, we are aware of the danger of romanticizing the pre-1994 struggle period and writing off important positive changes that have occurred

There is as yet no visible solution to the crisis in the South African trade union movement.

Fig 3.1: Environmental and internal changes in unions

Before 1994	After 1994
• Strong grassroots involvement (worker control) • Strong mobilization and contestation • Vibrant union structures • Strong layer of union leaders and activists • Social movement unionism • Vision for radical change of society • Easy to identify the enemy – employers and the apartheid state • Most unions driven by self-sacrifice and altruism • South African economy operated in isolation from world economy	• Decline of worker involvement in union affairs • Demobilization of union membership • Weak union structures • Brain drain (leaders and activists leaving for greener pastures) • Unions still active in politics but are now isolated from other movements • No clear vision of changing society • Not clear who the enemy is • Most unionists driven by individualism and a quest for upward mobility • South Africa now part of the global economy

since then. Therefore the table should be understood only as an indicator of trends of changes within the unions.

What can unions do?

Whereas many of the unions have taken advantage of the opportunities created by political liberalization, they are also aware of the constraints that democracy and globalization have introduced, and have been grappling with problems of lack of capacity for many years now. They are now professionalizing their approaches to organization and administration. For example, many unions now employ experts such as accountants, lawyers, researchers, managers, and health and safety experts to work in different areas of union work.

However, many of these innovations are producing unintended results. One of these is the emergence of new forms of segmentation in union employment. This is characterized by the emergence of a layer of powerful, well-paid officials at the top such as general secretaries, expert officials and managers of union investment companies, on the one hand, and the rest of the officials, particularly women, whose earnings and prospects for upward mobility are limited, on the other.

Several other initiatives are aimed at enhancing the capacity of the union movement to sustain its influence and to engage meaningfully with the challenges noted above. At the end of 1996 COSATU and FEDUSA jointly launched the Development Institute for Training, Support and Education for Labour (Ditsela). The Institute provides education and training for union leadership, with a strong emphasis on skills that are applicable in real situations in the union movement. In addition, COSATU has established a research centre, the National Labour and Economic Development Institute (Naledi), which provides research back-up to the federation and its affiliates.

However, the most ambitious initiative in recent years was COSATU's September Commission into the Future of Unions, which was asked to investigate and recommend strategies for the future of the federation and its affiliates. The Commission was a 12-member team of unionists and ex-unionists chaired by COSATU's then second vice-president, Connie September (hence the name). Its final report was published in August 1997 and it is one of the most detailed assessments of the problems facing the unions.

However, none of the initiatives undertaken thus far seems capable of taking the South African union movement out of its current crisis management mode. It seems likely, then, that the crisis will deepen as membership participation in union structures continues to decline and as power shifts from the hands of the rank and file into those of national leadership structures. As membership declines as a result of retrenchments, and as the ANC Government continues to promote neo-liberalism, the crisis for the unions will worsen further. The crisis has political, strategic, intellectual, and organizational dimensions and all of them have to be addressed if these unions are to avoid sliding into established and conservative 'sweetheart' unionism. (A sweetheart union is one which benefits from cooperating with the aims of capital or of particular employers.)

In this chapter we discussed trade unions and the role they play in trying to regulate workplace relations. We have shown that their ability to do this successfully is shaped by the transformation of work as discussed in chapter 1. Despite the obstacles that they had to overcome, the South African unions were successful in mobilizing for and winning concessions from employers and the state.

However, we have also noted that the union movement is showing signs of decline. Some might even say that the unions are developing oligarchic tendencies, as Robert Michels had predicted. What is clear is that the complexity of issues arising out of South Africa's double transition has forced the unions to become more professional in their methods of running their affairs. The theoretical issues raised in chapter 2 about bureaucracy and oligarchy in organizations are useful for broadening our understanding of these developments.

Conclusion: The Contested Future

In this book so far we have identified some of the organizations that shape, and are shaped by, the world of work. Our analysis draws on the foundational theorists of sociology. We show how the discipline emerged in order to understand the dislocating effects of industrialization on the world of work. We have paid particular attention to the theories of Marx, Weber, and Michels, and the key concepts they use: 'historical materialism'/'contestation', 'rationalization/bureaucratization', and 'oligarchy'.

At the core of this approach is a recognition of the dynamic interaction between the individual and society or (which is the same thing in slightly different words) the interaction between the 'global' and the 'local'. Let us consider how this interaction is viewed by different theoretical approaches.

It is possible to identify two broad responses to globalization: the sceptics and the radicals (Giddens 1999). The sceptics think nothing much has changed – it is all hype. 'It is', in the words of Michael Burawoy, summarizing the sceptical position, 'ideology rather than reality. The world is not that different today than earlier periods' (Burawoy 2000: 338). For many in the developing world 'globalization' is another manifestation of imperialism – the subordination of 'the South' within the world capitalist system. It is argued that we have had 'multinational companies' in southern Africa since the arrival of the Dutch East India Company (DEIC) in the middle of the seventeenth century. In other words there is no real need to think differently about the world of work in the era of globalization.

The second response is the mirror opposite. The radicals argue that everything has changed and see novelty everywhere. 'They believe,' Burawoy argues, 'that globalization is not just talk but refers to very real transformations that have dramatic consequences not only for the world economy but for the basic institutions of society – from sexuality to politics to the environment' (Burawoy 2000: 338). Nowhere is this more evident than in the work of Manuel Castells, who believes, as we showed in chapter 1, that we have entered into an entirely new phase of informational capitalism (Castells 1996).

But we are not persuaded by either approach, sceptic or radical. We would agree with Burawoy when he argues that what is required is a 'grounded globalization'. This is an approach which emphasizes the need to ground social analysis in a specific geographical and historical context. The context in this book is, of course, South Africa and southern Africa at the beginning of a new millennium. Grounded globalization, Buroway argues, is the remedy for the sceptics who ignore context and the radicals who ignore history (Burawoy 2000: 341–4). Our conclusion is that our future is a contested one, but it is a contest in which the 'local' increasingly interacts with the 'global'.

By grounding globalization in this way we are able to identify the co-existence in South Africa of old forms of work: the extractive industries of the old mining companies – such as Anglo American – side by side with the new, the innovative call centres which draw on information technology. What we see in South Africa, then, is a combination of 'the radical' view and 'the sceptics'' view of globalization – a process of continuity of the past, a process, which 'the radicals' ignore: combined with elements of the new, a process which 'the sceptics' deny. To understand this contradictory process of continuity and change, we need to ground globalization in the specific geographical and historical context of southern Africa.

What, then, of the future? We have suggested that the future is not something that is given, that is inevitable. The structures that shape our lives are social constructs, and are not as unchanging as the rising of the sun. Just as we create our social world, so we in turn can change it. But if we are to change the world it is necessary first to understand it.

We have suggested in chapter 1 that this world must be understood as containing contradictions that both close down options and also open up opportunities. We argue that post-Fordism has undermined militant industrial unionism. Simultaneously, however, globalization has opened up opportunities – through the Internet, email, and satellite television – of instant communication across the globe. This has enabled workers to organize transnational trade union strategies on an unprecedented scale. Furthermore the growth of new social movements in the South – mobilizing around land reform, anti-privatization, access to water and sanitation, resistance to electricity cut-offs – has opened up opportunities for new social alliances between labour and these social movements. We described this in chapter 3 as a form of social movement unionism.

In chapter 2 we suggested that the 'iron cage' of bureaucracy is being challenged by more flexible forms of post-Fordist and network organizations. But, we suggest, the claim that there is a shift to post-bureaucratic organization fails to take into account the difference in work organizations in various countries. Indeed, and contrary to post-Fordism trends, many organizations have seen the deepening of new forms of managerial control that are often accompanied by electronic surveillance such as that we see in call centres.

In chapter 3 we argued that there is evidence of Michels' iron law of oligarchy as unions become more professional and bureaucratic. It remains uncertain whether unions in South Africa will continue down this path and widen the gap between officials and members. Or whether a countermovement will emerge that re-establishes workplace democracy while simultaneously engaging in the new tripartite institutions that have been created. In other words, it is unclear whether the pendulum will swing, as Polanyi suggests it does over time in capitalist society, against the unregulated market back towards the social regulation of work (Polanyi 2001).

We have encapsulated the structure of the book and the contested nature of our future in the table below.

Book structure	Chapter 1: Work	Chapter 2: Organization	Chapter 3: Trade Unions
Key theorists	Karl Marx	Max Weber	Robert Michels
Key concepts	Historical materialism Contestation	Rationalization/ bureaucratization	Oligarchy
Theoretical approach	Continuing and contradictory transformation of work; as capital extends its control, it also lays the foundations for new forms of resistance.	Modern organizations evolved out of older traditional and charismatic forms. Modern bureaucracy has a hidden and an unstoppable logic.	Organizations have a strong tendency to bureaucratize. Leaders become alienated from their members. Hence, in unions, tensions develop between their mobilizing and contestatory role, on the one hand, and their bureaucratic and professional role, on the other.
Implications of the theoretical approach	Opportunities opening up and closing down; new winners and new losers.	The drive for bureau-cratization needs to be located in specific historical and social contexts.	In South Africa trade unions played a central role in the transition to democracy but these gains are being eroded by globalization.
The contested future	The fourth phase in the transformation of work has undermined militant industrial unionism, but globalization opens up opportunities for transnational trade union strategies linked to the new social movements.	Bureaucracy is being challenged by more flexible forms of post-Fordist and network organizations. But the new managerialism is attempting to assert a Taylorist type of control.	It remains uncertain as to whether unions will be able to re-establish their previous position in the workplace and in the formulation of economic and social policy.

The aim of this *Introduction to Sociology* series is to provide students with the tools for understanding society. A key question raised in this book is the way in which the nature of work and organizations is constantly changing. These changes create new winners and new losers.

The 'winners' in the new South Africa are those who have access to capital and skills that connect them to the global economy. They include:

- White business, particularly those who have 'globalized' their firms by investing their capital abroad and, in some cases, relocating their head offices.
- The rising black business class and the new political elite, who are the direct beneficiaries of black empowerment.
- The black and white middle and professional classes who have marketable skills.
- Those sections of the organized working class in the export sector of the economy who have relatively highly paid and secure jobs.

The 'losers' in the new South Africa are very similar to the losers in the old South Africa:
- The urban working poor, which includes those in casual jobs as well as the unemployed. A significant proportion of this category are young, that is between 16 and 30.
- The rural poor, especially women and the aged, who depend on a variety of livelihood strategies and state transfers such as pensions to survive.
- White workers who were protected but lacked skills in the old South Africa and now have to compete in a competitive labour market. They no longer have the welfare support they received from the apartheid state.

Globalization is polarizing the labour market, creating a small number of beneficiaries and a growing number of losers who are socially excluded and marginalized. The challenge facing South Africa is to turn these growing numbers of losers into winners. Without a significant proportion of the population benefiting from the creation of a democracy and the technological innovations of globalization, the future of the country will remain deeply contested.

Exercises

It has been an important concern of this book to present development material in a way that constitutes a number of ongoing themes. The exercises here continue that concern for coherent argument. Social Science is not about the recitation of hundreds of facts and figures. It is much more about the way that this material is ordered, argued, criticized, and mobilized. And, if it were necessary, there is a great deal of educational theory to support that approach (Ramsden 1992).

The exercises suggested below, then, are arranged from the simpler to the more challenging.

They come in different forms, some easier and some more difficult. The easier ones (let's call them **Level A** questions) typically ask you to do things such as:
*   'define' concepts;
*   'explain what' writer X says about something, or
*   'summarize' what writer Y says about something else.

This is relatively easy because it asks you simply to understand what a writer is saying and to express it in your own words.

Slightly more difficult questions (**Level B** questions) ask you to:
*   'explain how' A links to B according to Marx or Parsons;
*   'compare and contrast' modernization theory and dependency theory, or
*   'apply' modernization theory to a particular situation.

These questions take some extra thought because you are being asked to transpose ideas from one situation to another.

You may also be asked to:
*   'construct a careful argument about …'. In this case you are required to put together a coherent story which has logical and reasoned steps that follow from one another.

The most difficult, and the most interesting, questions (**Level C**) ask you to:
*   'construct your own examples of' a particular concept;
*   'discuss/critically evaluate' the ideas or the argument of theory A, or
*   'agree, or not, with' this or that view.

These are again more difficult because you have to start being creative and mobilize your own independent thoughts. They will also be somewhat longer questions because you will require further space to mobilize the steps of your argument. In the assessment of academic work, this skill is also considered the most valuable one.

Let us now consider some concrete examples from the material in this book.

Exercises

Level A

1 How would you define 'work'?
2 What are the main characteristics of pre-capitalist and capitalist forms of work?
3 List the four phases of work under capitalism and give two characteristics of each.
4 What are the assumptions underlying the systems approach to organizations?
5 What is an 'adhocracy'?
6 What is a 'trade union'?
7 What is the difference between a trade union and a movement?
8 What are the characteristics of Weber's ideal type bureaucracy?
9 What is an ideal type?

Level B

10 Why is work constantly being restructured ?
11 Why is Weber's notion of bureaucracy like a machine?
12 Compare and contrast the mainstream and critical approaches to organizations?
13 Why did Weber distrust 'the iron cage' of bureaucracy and what did he see as a solution to this distrust?
14 Compare and contrast Weber's 'iron cage of bureaucracy' with Michels's 'iron law of oligarchy'.
15 List the changes which have caused the decline of South African trade unions in the 1990s. Classify and group these changes variously as political, administrative, economic, globalization, cultural, etc.
16 Weber thought more and more organizations in modern society would adopt the bureaucratic model. Explain why he thought they would and then explain why this has not happened.

Level C

17 How does the process of changing work under capitalism link to Marx's notion of dialectical materialism?
18 Do you think a fourth phase in the restructuring of work is emerging and what implications does this have for trade unions?
19 Compare and contrast Marx's and Weber's approaches to sociology and to trade unions.
20 Do you agree that organizations need to become more flexible and what implications does this have for employees?
21 Critically discuss the role of globalization in the transformation of management and labour.
22 Evaluate the extent to which unions have changed under the impact of the 'double transition' in South Africa.

Annotated Bibliography

Adler, G, & E Webster (eds) (2000) *Trade Unions and Democratization in South Africa, 1985–1997* Johannesburg: Witwatersrand University Press.

> *The writings in this volume see labour as a collective actor capable of shaping democratization through the strategic use of power. The findings suggest that labour's marginalization could put the consolidation of democracy at risk.*

Giddens, A (2000) *Sociology* Cambridge: Polity Press.

> *This volume is a comprehensive introduction to sociology that emphasizes the significance of global developments in social life. See especially chapter 9 ('Groups and Organisations'), chapter 15 ('Work and Economic Life'), and chapter 16 ('The Globalisation of Social Life').*

Hall, S, D Held, & T McGrew (eds) (1992) *Modernity and its Futures* Cambridge: Polity Press in association with the Open University.

> *The book examines the forces reshaping modern industrial societies and the new patterns, structures, and relationships that are emerging in the contemporary world. Refer in particular to chapter 1 ('Liberalism, Marxism, and Democracy'), chapter 2 ('A Global Society?'), and chapter 4 ('Post-industrialism and Post-Fordism').*

Isaacs, S (2002) *South Africa in the Global Economy: Understanding the Challenges, Working Towards Alternatives* Durban: TURP, University of Natal.

> *This book tries to clarify the impact of global change on South Africa, highlighting the need to develop alternative, progressive responses to neo-liberalism.*

Jarvis, D (1999) *Making Sense of Workplace Restructuring* Durban: TURP, University of Natal.

> *This book examines why workplaces are being restructured. It looks at the opportunities and threats that this presents and at the strategies which unions can adopt to meet the challenges of restructuring.*

Thompson, P, & D McHugh (1995) *Work Organizations: A Critical Introduction* London: Macmillan Business.

> *This book breaks new ground by locating the major changes currently taking place in the world of work organizations in their historical, economic, and political contexts. It brings together and contrasts conventional and critical approaches from organizational analysis, management studies, labour process theory, and social psychology.*

Bibliography

Abrahamsson, B (1993) *The Logic of Organisations* London: Newbury Park; New Delhi: Sage.

Adler, G, & E Webster (eds) (2000) *Trade Unions and Democratization in South Africa, 1985–1997* Johannesburg: Witwatersrand University Press.

Beynon, H (1973) *Working for Ford* London: Allen Lane.

Braverman, H (1974) *Labour and Monopoly Capitalism: the Degradation of Work in the Twentieth Century* New York: Monthly Review Press.

Brown, R (1997) *The Changing Shape of Work* London: Macmillan Press Ltd.

Buhlungu, S (2001) 'The paradox of victory: South Africa's union movement in crisis' *New Labour Forum* 8.

Burawoy, M (1979) *Manufacturing Consent* Chicago: University of Chicago Press.

— (2000) *Global Ethnography: Forces, Connections, and Imaginations in a Postmodern World* Berkeley: University of California Press.

Castells, M (1996) *The Information Age: Economy, Society and Culture, the Rise of the Network Society* Oxford: Blackwell.

Clegg, S, C Hardy, & W Nord (1996) *Handbook of Organisation Studies* London: Sage.

Cohen, R (1994) 'Resistance and hidden forms of consciousness amongst African workers' in E Webster, L Alfred, L Bethlehem, A Joffe, & T Selikow (eds) *Work and Industrialisation in South Africa* Johannesburg: Ravan Press.

Crouch, C (1982) *Trade Unions: The Logic of Collective Action* London: Fontana.

Edwards, R (1979) *Contested Terrain: The Transformation of the Workplace in the Twentieth Century* New York: Basic Books.

Engels, F (1973) *The Conditions of the Working Class in England* Moscow: Progress Publishers.

Giddens, A (1999) *Run Away World*, Reith Lectures, London: British Broadcasting Corporation.

— (2000) *Sociology* Cambridge: Polity Press.

Gouldner, A (1954) *Patterns of Industrial Bureaucracy* Glencoe: Free Press.

— (1972) 'Bureaucracy is not inevitable' in P Worsley *For Sociology* Harmondsworth: Penguin.

Hall, S, D Held, & T McGrew (eds) (1992) *Modernity and its Futures* Cambridge: Polity Press in association with the Open University.

Haralambos, M, & M Holborn (1995) *Sociology: Themes and Perspectives*, 4th edition, London: Collins Educational.

Hyman, R (1971) *Marxism and the Sociology of Trade Unionism* London: Pluto.

Isaacs, S (2002) *South Africa in the Global Economy: Understanding the Challenges, Working Towards Alternatives* Durban: TURP, University of Natal.

Jarvis, D (1999) *Making Sense of Workplace Restructuring* Durban: TURP, University of Natal.

Joffe, A, D Kaplan, R Kaplinsky, & D Lewis (1995) *Improving Manufacturing Performance in South Africa: Report of the Industrial Strategy Project* Cape Town: University of Cape Town Press.

Johnstone, FA (1994) 'Class conflict and colour bars in the South African gold mining industry' in E Webster, L Alfred, L Bethlehem, A Joffe, & T Selikow (eds) *Work and Industrialisation in South Africa* Johannesburg: Ravan Press.

Kast, FE, & JE Rosenzweig (1979) *Organization Management: A Systems and Contingency Approach*, 3rd edition, New York: McGraw-Hill.

Kelly, J (1988) *Trade Unions and Socialist Politics* London/New York: Verso.

Kuckertz, H (1990) *Creating Order; the Image of the Homesteads in Mpondo Social Life* Johannesburg: Witwatersrand University Press.

Lan, P (2001) 'The body as a contested terrain for labour control: cosmetic retailers in department stores and direct selling' in R Baldoz, C Koeber, & P Kraft (eds) *The Critical Study of Work: Labor Technology and Global Production* Philadelphia: Temple University Press.

Lester, RA (1958) *As Unions Mature* Princeton: Princeton University Press.

Lipset, SM, M Trow, & J Coleman (1956) *Union Democracy: The Internal Politics of the International Typographical Union* New York: Anchor Books.

Macdonald, CL, & C Sirianni (1996) *Working in the Service Society* Philadelphia: Temple University Press.

Marx, K (1976) *Capital: A Critique of Political Economy*, Volume 1, Penguin Books: London.

Michels, R (1959) *Political Parties: A Sociological Study of the Emergence of Leadership, the Psychology of Power, and Oligarchic Tendencies of Organizations* New York: Dover Publications.

Mintzberg, H (1983) *Structure in Fives: Designing Effective Organisations* New Jersey: Prentice Hall.

Morgan, G (1997) *Images of Organization* London. Sage.

Offe, C (1985) 'Work: the key sociological category?' in C Offe *Disorganised Capitalism: Contemporary Transformation of Work and Politics* Cambridge: Polity Press.

Pahl, RE (1984) *Divisions of Labour* Oxford: Blackwell Publishers.

Phakathi, S (2002) `Self-directed work teams in a post-apartheid goldmine: perspectives from the rock face' *Journal of Workplace Learning* 14 (7).

Piore, M, & C Sabel (1984) *The Second Industrial Divide: Possibilities for Prosperity* New York: Basic Books.

Polanyi, K (2001) *The Great Transformation: The Political and Economic Origins of Our Time* Boston: Beacon Press.

Reed, M (1992) *The Sociology of Organisations* Hemel Hempstead: Harvester.

September Commission (1997) *September Commission Report* Johannesburg: COSATU.

Taylor, FW (1947) *Scientific Management* New York and London: Harper & Row.

Thompson, EP (1963) *The Making of the English Working Class* London: Penguin Books.

Thompson, P (1989) *The Nature of Work: An Introduction to Debates on the Labour Process*, 2nd edition, London: Macmillan.

Thompson, P, & D McHugh (1995) *Work Organisations: A Critical Introduction* London: Macmillan Business.

Von Holdt, K (2000). 'From the politics of resistance to the politics of reconstruction? The union and "ungovernability" in the workplace' in G Adler & E Webster *Trade Unions and Democratization in South Africa, 1985–1997* London: Macmillan.

Voss, K, & R Sherman (2000) 'Breaking the iron law of oligarchy: union revitalization in the American labor movement' *American Journal of Sociology* 106 (2).

Weber, M (1968) *Economy and Society: An Outline of Interpretive Sociology*, volumes 1–3, New York: Bedminster Press.

Webster, E (1985) *Cast in a Racial Mould: Labour Process and Trade Unionism in the Foundries* Johannesburg: Ravan.

— (1994) 'The rise of social movement unionism: two faces of the Black trade union movement in South Africa' in E Webster, L Alfred, L Bethlehem, A Joffe, & T Selikow (eds) *Work and Industrialisation in South Africa* Johannesburg: Ravan Press.

— (2002) 'South Africa' in D Cornfield & R Hodson (eds) *Worlds of Work: Building an International Sociology of Work* New York: Kluwer Academic/ Plenum Publishers.

Webster, E, & G Adler (1999) 'Towards a class compromise in South Africa's "double transition": bargained liberalization and the consolidation of democracy' *Politics and Society* 27 (3): 347–85.

Glossary

Adhocracy: an organizational form which moulds itself to various situations

Critical/Marxist approach to organization: an approach which sees organizations as sites of conflict between ruling classes and working classes. Organizations here are instruments of domination used by the ruling class or employers

Deskilling: the process under capitalism by which workers lose their specialized crafts and expertise, and work is broken down into ever smaller and simpler parts

Emotional labour: 'the conscious manipulation of the worker's self-presentation, either to display feeling states and/or to create feeling states in others' (Macdonald & Sirianni 1996: 3)

Fordism: work organization based on two principles: the integration of different parts of the labour process by a system of conveyors; and the fixing of workers to jobs and positions determined by the assembly line

Formal rationality: the tendency in bureaucracies to focus on technical procedures and rules rather than broader organizational aims, that is 'red tape'

Functional flexibility: an aspect of post-Fordist work organization where workers can perform a number of different tasks. This may involve increasing the number of skills a worker has (*multi-skilling*), or it may simply involve increasing the number of tasks to be done (*multi-tasking*)

Globalization radicals: theorists who maintain that modern globalization is dramatically different from anything in the past, and that it is reshaping our world quite significantly

Globalization skeptics: theorists who say that modern globalization is nothing new, and that nothing much has changed

Globalization: the growing interdependence and linkage of various parts of the world, also 'the compression of time and space'

Grounded globalization: theorists who say that modern globalization is neither radically new nor more of the same, but that each situation will have its own mixture of the new and the old

Ideal type: a mental model of the way various attributes of a phenomenon logically fit together, although it does not exist in reality

Localization: the impact that local circumstances will have on the broader trends of globalization

Michels' iron law of oligarchy: Robert Michels' view that organizations inevitably become dominated by a small, powerful elite pursuing their own interests

Network organization: an organization which continually reshapes itself to new situations, including or excluding parts as needed

Network society: a society shaped by network organizations (see 'Network organization' above)

Numerical flexibility: an aspect of post-Fordist work organization where there are groups of workers who have no job security. Such workers are employed as temporary, contract, casual, or part-time workers to make the labour market more 'flexible'

Post-Fordism/flexible specialization: a work organization which is able to change its products very rapidly. Based on functional flexibility and numerical flexibility (see 'Numerical flexibility')

Proletarianization: the process under capitalism by which peasants are pushed into wage labour by losing their access to productive resources such as land and livestock

Redistributive mode of production: a society in pre-colonial times where people lived on the land and shared what they produced

Social movement: a coordinated attempt by a group of people to achieve a common goal. A movement is characterized by an informality of organization and a weakness or absence of hierarchical structures.

Social movement unionism: trade union action across two fronts: one economic in trying to achieve increases and improvements in wages and condition, the other political in acting as a voice for its members on social and political issues

Substantive rationality: a concern in organizations with 'the values and desired end of an action' rather than the technical rules or formal rationality

Systems/functionalist approach to organization: an approach which sees organizations as harmonious patterns with smoothly interacting parts, much like a human body

Taylorism/scientific management: work organization based on the dictation to the worker of the precise manner in which work is to be performed

Weber's iron cage of bureaucracy: Max Weber's notion that modern society is inevitably caught in machine-like bureaucratic organizations

Work: a social activity where an individual or group puts in effort during a specific time and space, sometimes with the expectation of monetary – or other kinds of – rewards, or with no expectation of reward, but with a sense of obligation to others

Index